Viktor Frankl's Logotherapy

Viktor Frankl's Logotherapy

Method of Choice in Ecumenical Pastoral Psychology

Ann V. Graber

Wyndham Hall Press
2004

Viktor Frankl's Logotherapy:
Method of Choice in Ecumenical Pastoral Psychology

Ann V. Graber

The Rhodes-Fulbright Library

Permissions for use of copyrighted materials are acknowledged on the facing page.

Book Design by Matthew D. J. Kies
Cover Design by Mark S. McCullough
Cover photograph courtesy of NASA

ISBN: 1-55605-364-9
Library of Congress Control Number: 2004102787

WYNDHAM HALL PRESS
Lima, Ohio 45806
www.wyndhamhallpress.com

Printed in The United States of America

PERMISSIONS

The author gratefully acknowledges the following who gave their permission to use excerpts from their material:

Helen Gennari for interview and reprint of excerpts from "Logotherapy in Today's Managed Care Climate" (IFL, 1999, 27-30).

Elisabeth Lukas for her gracious permission to quote from her book, *Meaningful Living* (1984, pp. 21, 27-28, 73).

George E. Naff for the generous use of his meticulously compiled "Glossary of Logotherapeutic Terms and Phrases" (unpublished).

Thomas J. Peterson for permission to extrapolate from his article, "Frankl and Jung on Meaning" (IFL, 1992, 33-40).

George Rice for reprint of his PowerPoint slide, "Symbol for Logotherapy."

George Rice, Michael Pitts, Julius Rogina, Irmeli Sjolie for permission to include passages from our jointly written course, *Franklian Psychology: Meaning-Centered Interventions* (2002).

Julius M. Rogina for permission to include the "Rogina Model for Treating Violent Behaviors" as presented in the seminar course, *Viktor Frankl's Logotherapeutic Model of Mental Health* (2000).

The Perseus Book Group for permission to quote excerpts from *Recollections: An Autobiography by Viktor Frankl* (Frankl, V. E., 1997, p. 82-83).

To the
Logos
in each of us

CONTENTS

LIST of FIGURES

ACKNOWLEDGEMENTS

A work of this scope is not a solitary undertaking, but the result of enduring support and encouragement from many. My particular appreciation is extended to:

Dr. Viktor Frankl, who provided the inspiration and the incentive "to find meaning in life by helping others find meaning in their lives."

Prof. Ewert Cousins, my dissertation advisor par excellence, whose phenomenal grasp of world spirituality induced me to learn more, and whose human kindness sustained me through this research project.

Dr. John Morgan, whose visionary foresight saw the potential of this work for pastoral psychology and related fields, and who caused it to become a published book.

My logotherapy colleagues, particularly Dr. Robert Barnes, President of the Viktor Frankl Institute of Logotherapy, George Rice, Julius Rogina, Michael Pitts, Irmeli Sjolie, Connie Sweeny, and James Yoder.

My teachers, instructors, professors, and mentors—from Kindergarten through doctoral studies—who helped me to reach this educational and professional summit.

My students through the years whose thirst for knowledge has challenged me to keep on learning.

My clients who taught me much about the human condition and the indomitable courage of the human spirit.

My fellow travelers through life: family and friends, who have stood by my side in times of tribulation and celebration.

With deep gratitude,
Ann V. Graber, PhD

FOREWORD

Ann Graber has written a study that can add a new chapter to our understanding of psychotherapy and its place in Western culture. The story of Sigmund Freud is well known, along with his founding with Alfred Adler of the psychoanalytic movement in Vienna at the beginning of the 20th century. What is not so well-known is the role played by another Viennese psychotherapist, Viktor Frankl, whose life spanned almost the entirety of the 20th century. It is true that Frankl is known to many readers from his book, *Man's Search for Meaning,* (1959), the gripping story of his survival in Nazi concentration camps. But not equally well known is the school of psychotherapy that he founded which was validated by that harrowing experience. In the midst of his overwhelming suffering he had an insight into the creative capacity of the human spirit in time of crisis that Freud and the early members of his psychoanalytic circle had not directly explored.

Freud, who had been trained in the medical world of Vienna, looked into the depths of the psyche of his patients and discovered there a dynamism by which the psyche—with the aid of a guide—could heal itself. In a parallel way, but drawing from a higher level, Frankl, in the midst of excruciating suffering looked deep into the human spirit and discovered there the courage not only to survive, but to live life on a higher spiritual level. It was this experience of awakening to the power and transcendence of the human spirit that has energized Viktor Frankl's logotherapy movement that Ann Graber describes in this book.

For this challenging task, Ann draws from her rich cultural heritage and educational background, her years of professional experience as a psychotherapist, and her deep insight into the creative possibilities of Viktor Frankl's logotherapy for the realm of pastoral psychology. She has presented her case with impressive clarity that can benefit psychotherapists, particularly the group of professionals who work in the fields of religion, spirituality, and pastoral counseling. Her book is strong in its treatment of its three major areas: (1) the historical background and the philosophical currents of logotherapy at the time of its emergence; (2) her knowledge of logotherapy as a psychological method and as a professional community; (3) her original insights into the role of logotherapy in the present and future milieu of ecumenical pastoral psychology.

Ann situates the schools of Freud, Adler, and Frankl within the context of the history of Austrian culture during the past 100 years. Her early education was in the Austrian Tyrol. Later she studied in Vienna and absorbed the cultural richness of that milieu. Having grown up in the later unfolding of this culture, she knows the milieu firsthand. In her writing, she conveys a sense of cultural familiarity that I have not found in my many years of contact with the psychoanalytic community in New York. Equipped with this cultural awareness, she effectively presents the philosophical and cultural context of the psychology of Freud, Adler, and Frankl.

Over the course of many years she has received the extensive training necessary to qualify her as a logotherapist and pastoral psychologist. This has led to her becoming very active in the professional work of the logotherapy community. Since earning the Diplomate credential from the Viktor Frankl Institute of Logotherapy, she has been continually involved in training logotherapists, and in organizing educational seminars, initiating the distance learning program for the Institute in the United States and participating in logotherapy conferences in the United States and abroad. This achievement gives an authoritative voice to the chapters of her book dealing with the concepts, orientation, and methods of logotherapy.

With her professional involvement in logotherapy as a background, Ann, in the final section of her book, presents her own contribution to the logotherapy movement: her identifying and highlighting the distinctive contribution that logotherapy can make in the larger field of psychotherapy. With concrete examples from her own practice, she highlights the fact that Viktor Frankl's therapy deals not with a long process of psychotherapy, as is the case with Freudian analysis, but with situations in which spiritual values are awakened and harnessed to aid the client to deal effectively with the current crisis.

The examples from her practice dramatically illustrate the distinctive contribution that logotherapy can make and convincingly established the central claim of her work: that logotherapy is the method of choice for pastoral psychology. It is often the case that pastoral counseling takes place in hospitals and in traumatic situations which need to be addressed at once. Logotherapy is uniquely able to deal with such situations effectively and can open the door to other types of therapy and spiritual guidance over a long range process.

This is a book that all should read, for it fills in a chapter of our own cultural history and gives dramatic testimony to the capacity of the human spirit not only to transcend traumatic experiences but to illumine our search for meaning.

Ewert H. Cousins, Ph.D.
Professor Emeritus, Theology
Fordham University
General Editor, *World Spirituality: An Encyclopedic History of the Religious Quest*

INTRODUCTION

Before Freud, questions having to do with "the meaning of life" were brought before the minister, priest, pastor, or rabbi, and, perhaps, were asked of the philosopher. After Freud, they tended to be asked on the psychoanalyst's couch. As the science of psychotherapy grew and developed, boundaries were drawn and redrawn as specialties evolved and staked their professional turf. Psychiatry now tends to be concerned primarily with psycho-pharmacology; salvation of the soul is seen as the purview of religion; and psychology is preoccupied with testing and assessing.

Who is there to tend to the psycho-spiritual needs of the people? Pastoral Psychology, a fairly new and green branch on the tree of human services, is trying to fill the gap between medical and religious functions. Its tool kit needs more fitting tools for the task than those that were crafted by medical science, psychology, or theology. The unique contribution of this study will be to devise a treatment model for Pastoral Psychology that is spiritually based and psychologically sound. It will be a timely instrument to meet contemporary and future needs of professionals who endeavor to meet the psycho-spiritual needs of those who seek their services.

To that end the philosophy and spiritually based psychotherapy of Viktor Emil Frankl, M.D., Ph.D., termed *logotherapy*, has been found to offer the greatest potential. The tenets of logotherapy will be explored and compiled to culminate in concrete treatment models with wide application in practice.

After a substantive exposition of the theoretical formulations, and establishing relevance of Franklian theory to Pastoral Psychology, logotherapeutic treatment approaches applicable to most pastoral counseling situations—excluding the pathology of mental illness—will be presented.

Logotherapy's inherent ecumenical posture will be highlighted as well as its efficacy for interfaith counseling. The work is intended to meet the needs of professionals using pastoral psychology who work in the "global village" with its divergent faith traditions and cultural values. The primary focus will be on accessing the intrinsic human spirit in order to bring about meaningful change that leads to psycho-spiritual wellbeing.

The corpus of material by Viktor Frankl will be supplemented by other scholars of logotherapy and resources from theology, psychology, counseling, and related fields. Together it will serve to ground the work in the spirit of hopefulness as well as in psychological soundness. Poets and mystics will be occasionally invited to make guest appearances on the pages of this book to enhance given points and to add their grace and blessings.

Ann V. Graber
St. Louis, MO 2004

Please note: Viktor Frankl wrote and taught in an era before "inclusive language" was a mandate. In that context "man" is used as a generic term for human being; "mankind" implies humankind; "he" stands for he or she. Since the intention of this study was to present a concise rendering of Viktor Frankl's logotherapy, his linguistic style has been retained.

I

HISTORICAL OVERVIEW

Synopsis of Politico-Social Milieu of Vienna

It is well to consider the ethos or the inherent characteristics of a society, and the prevailing spirit of the times, when looking for the dynamic that produced a better understanding of human nature. Although it could have happened anywhere, history records that psychotherapy arose in Vienna and that it began in the days of Sigmund Freud. A closer look at the historical background and the social environment where the science of the human psyche arose may give us a better insight why it happened as it did.

In the latter part of the nineteenth century and the first decade of the twentieth, Vienna was the old Imperial city. It was the capital of the Austro-Hungarian Empire, seat of the emperors of the House of Habsburg, who had ruled since establishing their reign in Austria in 1278. Vienna was the cultural Mecca to the people living in the far-flung provinces that comprised the empire. With a population of over two million people, Vienna was the second largest city on the European continent, second only to Paris. It was a German speaking political stronghold, a major economic center, and citadel of learning that attracted many notables in the field of music, art, literature, and the sciences; it also attracted thousands of immigrants from the provinces and beyond—Freud's family among them. As the capital city of an empire of sixty million people, it was the administrative hub, the center of learning where the arts flourished side by side with the sciences (Gould, 1993, 1-2).

The greatest flowering of Austrian culture coincided with its political decline. The reigning monarch at the time was Kaiser Franz Josef (Emperor Francis Joseph) who had ascended to the throne in 1847. Even though political unrest had been seething beneath the surface for some time, the end of Austria's political power and influence came fairly suddenly. A shot fired in Sarajevo, in 1914, killing Archduke Franz Ferdinand, heir to the throne, plunged Austria and the world into the First World War. The old emperor died in 1916, while the country was at war. The political decline reached its nadir in 1918. A defeated Austria signed an armistice with the Allies stripping it of much of its former holdings, and reducing Austria to one tenth of its former size. Shortly thereafter, the monarchy was overthrown and Austria became a republic. With WW-I ended not only the monarchy, but also a lifestyle that had been conducive to cultural pursuits.

The armistice of 1918 brought harsh deprivations to the Austrian people, particularly those living in the largest city of the former empire, Vienna. Austria had severe economic and political problems following WW-I. The economic problems were exacerbated by the world wide depression of the late 1920s and the 1930s. Austria's political problems centered on conflicts between two political parties, each with its own army. The central political issue was whether to keep Austria independent or to unite Austria with Germany. This internal conflict raged until 1938 when German troops seized Austria and Hitler announced the *Anschluss* (annexation) of Austria and Germany. Austria's fate thus became tied to that of Nazi Germany, whose quest for power led to WW-II in 1939. The Allies (comprised of the United States, the United

Kingdom, France, the Soviet Union, and other nations) finally defeated Germany and Austria in 1945.

After the war, a coalition government helped stabilize an Austria that was divided into American, British, French, and Russian zones of occupation. In 1955, the Allies ended their occupation of the country. To obtain its independence, Austria agreed to be permanently neutral—that is, completely uninvolved in international military affairs. As a neutral nation, Austria became an important channel for the exchange of ideas between the non-Communist countries of Western Europe and the Communist countries of Eastern Europe. Vienna gradually resumed a position in the international community by becoming the home of a number of UN agencies (McGrath, "Austria," 2001).

With the restoration of its war-damaged cultural edifices and the rebuilding of its transportation systems Austria became again a favored attraction. Even though its political influence is now insignificant compared to its former days, the cultural influence it still exerts is considerable. For example, the re-opening of the bomb-damaged Vienna Opera House, in 1955, was a world-gala event; the Salzburg music festivals have upheld the banner of excellence for classical music and draw audiences from around the word; Austrian skiers have played a large part in developing and popularizing Alpine skiing worldwide.

Parallels Between the Tides of History and Waves of Psychological Theories

It is said that "the times produce the man." One might also wonder if a place is propitious to the birth of new ideas and ideals. However the case may be, Vienna was the place that saw the birth of psychoanalysis and the subsequent development of two other

Viennese schools of psychotherapy. The theories of each of these three schools, and the problems they addressed, parallel the country's history and reflect the mood and the experience of its people, particularly of their capital city, Vienna.

A Viennese, Stephen Kalmar, gives us an on-site observer's view of the changing political and cultural currents of Vienna during those times. Growing up during the Austro-Hungarian Monarchy, Kalmar knew the Imperial Vienna—the city of Freud. He also witnessed the tumultuous years subsequent to the fall of the Habsburg Empire, the struggle for freedom and the search for identity—the city of Adler. He furthermore experienced Vienna when the search for meaning in the midst of chaos was paramount—the city of Frankl (1982, xv - xxiv). The history of a new school of thought is, in its first phase, largely the history of its founder. A closer look at the historical and cultural milieu of the founders of the three Viennese schools of psychotherapy and their corresponding ideologies will bear this out.

Sigmund Freud, born in 1856, was a child of the monarchy. He lived and worked in a tradition-bound, paternalistic, authoritarian, autocratic, hierarchically structured society. That was true of the home, where father ruled as head of the house; in school, where teachers laid down the law and meted out punishment; the state, where the Kaiser ruled supreme over his subjects; and church, where God ruled over his universe and had to be obeyed. Freedom of expression was not tolerated. Therefore, all that remained unexpressed went into hiding in the subconscious and festered as repression. Life appeared orderly on the surface, yet there was subconscious ferment and rebellion brewing. Repression of authentic feelings often presented symptomatically as hysteria, which was socially more acceptable than disagreement with the status quo of the society. By and large, this was the condition of the patients Dr.

Freud would have encountered: human beings living with external and internal repression. Dealing with this phenomenon led Freud to uncover the subconscious, explore its content of drives and instincts and their reaction formations, and helped him to formulate his theory of ***Psychoanalysis***—giving birth to the first Viennese school of psychotherapy.

Alfred Adler came to professional prominence almost a generation later and faced a different set of circumstances. Those first few years after the end of the First World War were years of great soul-searching in Austria, both individually and collectively as a nation. The Habsburg Empire, having played an important role in Europe for many centuries, had collapsed, creating an "existential vacuum," which the new Austrian republic was attempting to fill. An empire of sixty million people had been reduced to a small nation of six million. Vienna's magnificent educational, cultural, and economic institutions—the universities, academies, theaters, operas and concert halls, the publishing houses, banks and insurance companies, administrative and industrial complexes—were to serve one-tenth of the population they had served before. Out of the six million Austrians, two million still lived in Vienna as before, a swollen head for that small body. Every Austrian had to confront the task of readjusting his or her life to the new situation. What did life mean for the large number of aristocrats now that the emperor's court was gone? What did life mean for the equally large number of well-educated professors, state officials, writers, musicians, and other artists? Kalmar describes his countrymen as follows:

> The majority of Austrians were strongly conservative, religious, mostly Catholic, looking for ways to preserve their old values, their traditions. In opposition to these conservative Austrians who formed the government were the

> Social Democrats, concentrated in Vienna, who saw it as their task to form a liberal, socialistic, and anti-traditional society, with equal rights for all leading to freedom of opinion, freedom from dogmas, freedom for academic research. This, to the Social Democrats, was to be the new meaning of life in the new Austria (1982, xvi-xviii).

As we can see from the above depiction this was a society in transition with values in collision. The very foundation of the established order had been profoundly shaken, if not demolished, on every front. What had been solid and dependably there, was suddenly gone. A new order was in the making but did not have solidity yet. Adler understood the needs of his patients and compatriots during these times of uncertainty and soul-searching, and broke away from Freud's reductionistic, cause and effect interpretation of the human person with its focus on sexual repression.

Alfred Adler had been one of Freud's most important disciples. Freud had even considered him the "heir apparent" of the psychoanalytic movement at one time. But Adler later rebelled against Freud's theory of total biological and environmental determination. Having done some medical research independently he did not concur with some assumptions postulated by Freud. Adler was looking for an expanded psychological framework which would allow more freedom to forge individual identity. Feeling disempowered, individually and collectively, his contemporaries were in search of an identity and empowerment. Adlerian concepts suited the conditions and aspirations prevailing in the Vienna of the 1920s and 1930s very well. Adler went on to establish his ***Individual Psychology***—giving rise to the second Viennese school of psychotherapy.

Meanwhile, a boy was growing up in Vienna, a precocious child. Born during the monarchy, ***Viktor Emil Frankl*** was nine years old when WW-I broke out. He saw much hardship during the four years of the war and witnessed the turmoil and chaos attendant to the post WW-I era in his native city. In later years he would recall the privations they suffered. He remembered having been sent to visit with relatives during summers in Moravia in order to have something to eat. These experiences made an indelible impression on the young Viktor. He gained an empathy for the suffering (Gould, 1993, 2-3).

In 1920, when Viktor Frankl was 15 years old, the 64-year-old Sigmund Freud dominated the psychological scene internationally. Meanwhile, young Viktor, not being an athletic youngster, spent his time reading and attending lectures in many subjects that interested him: natural sciences, philosophy, and especially psychology. In his teens, we find an amazingly "old beyond his years" young man. Before graduating from high school, Viktor Frankl had followed Freud's theories; he had even corresponded with the great Dr. Freud, who promptly answered the boy's letters. But new concepts were formulating in young Viktor's fertile mind. His idea, which grew into a conviction, that individuals had to find their own meaning in life, differed sharply from Freud's pandeterministic views, the view that we are totally determined by heredity and environment.

When Frankl entered the University of Vienna to start his medical studies, he first considered becoming a dermatologist or a gynecologist, but later decided to become a psychiatrist. Already in his first year at the university, Frankl, who had become a Social Democrat (like Adler) became president of the Social Democratic student movement in 1924. Frankl was attracted to Adler and his Association for Individual Psychology and became one of its youngest members. A few years after joining the Association of Individual Psychology, Frankl had become well-known and well-liked in that group. He was invited to read papers at meetings—among them the 1926 International Congress for Individual Psychology in Düsseldorf, Germany, when only twenty-one years of age. In this paper, and more so later on, Frankl developed ideas that were to some extent outside the traditional framework of Adler's system of thought. Soon after, Frankl encountered the works of the philosopher and phenomenologist Max Scheler, which had a profound influence on the development of his logotherapy (Kalmar, 1982, p. xix).

Viktor Frankl continued reading, studying, and developing his philosophy. While preparing for his life work in psychiatry, ominous clouds were gathering on the horizon: soon the world would be gripped in the Great Depression and its aftermath. Following the collapse of the stock market in 1929, inflation was rampant, unemployment rose sharply, and the suicide rate soared. Especially the young seemed hopeless and despairing, questioning the meaning of their existence. Frankl rose to the challenge of working with these distraught youths psychotherapeutically.

In 1930, Frankl began to set up youth counseling centers in Austrian cities, primarily for students and the unemployed. He lectured extensively for organizations of the socialist youth movement in Austria, and as far as Berlin, Prague, and Budapest. His theme revolved increasingly around the meaning of life. By 1933, he had systematized his ideas and talked about logotherapy—treatment through finding "meaning." He taught that we can "wrest meaning from life by turning suffering into a human triumph" (Frankl, 1997, p. 64).

By this time he no longer belonged to the Adlerian Society. Once the "favorite son" of that circle, he was asked to leave when his ideas deviated from Adler's. Just as Adler had left Freud's *Psychoanalysis* to found his own school of thought, Frankl in turn left Adler's *Association of Individual Psychology* to found the third Viennese school of psychotherapy—***Existential Analysis*** and ***Logotherapy***.

Birth and Development of Psychotherapy

For thousands of years, humankind has been aware of existing in different ontological dimensions: the visible, tangible, material form—called body; and the invisible, intangible, non-material aspect of being—variously referred to as the mind or psyche. Historically, philosophy had grappled with the mind/body concept, and religion had tried to explain it. At the beginning of the 20th century yet another attempt was made to understand this non-somatic dimension of our being, the psyche. Leading the exploration on the frontiers of the psyche was the Austrian physician, Sigmund Freud. Medicine at that time had a mechanistic Newtonian/Cartesian approach to healing. The human body was treated as a complex biochemical machine. Little attention was paid to what *animated* this "machine." The patient was viewed as an object in need of repair.

Sigmund Freud (1856-1939)

Sigmund Freud was the first modern day physician who looked beyond the physical organism to a dimension that was non-material: the conscious, subconscious, and unconscious mind or psyche. Freud discovered an important connection between health and well-being and the dynamics operative in the psyche. He discovered that certain physical sicknesses can originate in the psychological dimension, especially when the will to pleasure—particularly sexual pleasure—is repressed into the unconscious where it can cause neurosis, hysteria, and physical illness. This gave rise to Freud's theory of the "pleasure principle" or *will to pleasure*. In fact, in Freud's time sex was repressed, even on a mass level. This was a consequence of puritanism, and this puritanism was predominant in Anglo-Saxon countries. Small wonder that it was these countries that proved to be most receptive to Freud's psychoanalysis—and resistant to those schools of psychotherapy that went beyond Freud (Frankl, 1988, p.12).

Freud showed the crucial importance of unconscious thinking to all human thought and activity. His work on the origin and treatment of mental illness helped form the basis of modern psychiatry. Freud greatly influenced the field of abnormal psychology and the study of the personality. His theories on sexual development led to open discussion and treatment of sexual matters and problems. Freud's emphasis on the importance of childhood helped teach the value of giving children an emotionally nourishing environment. His insights also influenced the fields of anthropology and sociology. Most social scientists accept his concept that an adult's social relationships are patterned after early family relationships (Decker, "Freud," 2001).

It is important to consider that Freud found himself constrained by the very nature of his work, and that his subsequent conclusions were drawn from observations of his patients. The healthy and well-adjusted did not need to seek the services of a psychiatrist. Therefore, the earliest theories of personality development were based on observations of abnormal development and abnormal functioning. Surprisingly, a century later they still prevail. Particularly in North America, the psychoanalytic and psychodynamic orientation is still a dominant influence.

Since Freud was a man with enormous influence in the medical world of his time, his theories and his psychoanalytic approach to mental health spread quickly—becoming the foundation for the new science that probed the depth of the human psyche and changed the way we perceive ourselves. In an interesting text on the thinking of Western culture, titled *From Freud to Frankl*, John H. Morgan states:

> The impact that Freud's thought has had upon Western culture in the last 75 years is profound. Since the Publication of his *Die Traumdeutung*, 1900 (*The Interpretation of Dreams*, 1955), Freud's thought has gained such widespread usage that it would be difficult to imagine a modern world devoid of his contributions to the understanding of the individual in society. If his studies of the human psyche have revolutionized man's thoughts about and attitudes toward the unconscious, his writings on religion, society, and culture have shaken older images of human experiences and ushered in a new era of religious and social theorizing (Morgan, 1987, p. 2).

Viktor Frankl pays the highest tribute to Sigmund Freud. He alludes to Freud's place in history through a story that is told at the oldest synagogue of the world, Prague's medieval Alt Neu Synagogue. When the guide there shows the interior, he tells visitors that the seat once occupied by the famous Rabbi Loew has never been taken over by any of his followers; another seat has been set up for them because Rabbi Loew could never be replaced, no one could match him. For centuries no one was allowed to sit down on his seat. Frankl declares, "The chair of Freud should also be kept empty" (Frankl, 1988, p. 12).

Alfred Adler (1870-1937)

Beyond Freud, further insight into the human psyche was gained by Alfred Adler, a favorite colleague of Freud at the University of Vienna from 1902 to 1911. Adler was one of the most brilliant psychiatrists and psychotherapists of the Twentieth Century. In Europe, Adlerian psychology became the most widely followed. Adler moved to New York City in 1934 and his influence spread in the New World as well. Historian Hannah S. Decker, in an online article on Adler, states:

> ***Adler, Alfred*** (1870-1937), Austrian psychiatrist, developed important theories concerning the motivation of human behavior. According to Adler, the major force of all human activity is a striving from a feeling of inferiority toward perfection. Adler at first referred to this force as an *aggressive drive*. He later called the force a *striving for superiority*. Adler termed his school of thought *individual psychology*. Today, it is often referred to as *Adlerian psychology* (Decker, "Adler," 2001).

The young science of psychotherapy was evolving and was being developed into a distinct medical specialty, psychiatry. Since the fathers of psychotherapy, notably Freud and Adler, were medically trained men, they brought the same prevailing mechanistic orientation to the exploration of the human psyche and to the development of psychiatry and psychotherapy. Thanks to Freud, a psychological dimension was recognized to exist beyond the physical. This added a new dimension to the treatment of a patient; however, at the same time the human spirit was ignored or forgotten by this new medical specialty. This was the state of the art when Frankl arrived on the scene.

The foregoing is, of course, a vast oversimplification of Freud and Adler's contributions to psychotherapy. It is intended only to delineate the historical development that led from Freud to Adler to Frankl.

Viktor Frankl was born in Vienna in 1905. Since early childhood he sensed a depth to life, and pondered its meaning. He was an intellectually precocious child. As we learned previously, even before finishing high school, he had begun a scientific correspondence with Sigmund Freud. Later, as a medical student, Frankl became a member of the inner circle of Alfred Adler. While Frankl credited Freud with finding new insights into human nature, and Adler with enriching the field, he felt that neither Freud's concept of the human being motivated by a *drive for pleasure*, nor Adler's theory that we are motivated by a *drive for power*, adequately addressed the totality of being human (Fabry, 1987, 7-8).

Appreciating what his great teachers had taught him, he was later fond of saying, "Even a dwarf standing on the shoulders of a giant, can see farther than the giant himself." This was the background, the milieu from which ***Viktor Frankl*** stepped forth to formulate his own psychotherapy, ***Existential Analysis*** and ***Logotherapy***, which is characterized by a *will to meaning*.

☙

With all due respect to the luminaries of history, we must see them in the light of their times, within their historical context. So it is with the founders of schools of psychotherapy. As we have seen, Freud stepped upon the stage of history in a time very different from Adler's, who was his junior by 14 years; and, distinctly different from Frankl's time, born 35 years after Adler.

Freud had the luxury of making his painstaking observations and establishing his career during the relatively stable times before WW-I. In times of little change, tradition is a reliable guide and values are held in common by society. Freud's early major works, *Traumdeutung* (*The Interpretation of Dreams*, 1900) and *Totem and Taboo* (1912), were written before the turmoil that was to come engulf his part of the world. He dealt largely with the attitudes and values prevalent in the Victorian era because his patients were steeped in those attitudes.

Viktor Frankl in his book, *The Unconscious God*, quotes the Viennese poet, Arthur Schnitzler, as saying that there are only three virtues: "objectivity, courage, and a sense of responsibility." Frankl muses that it would be tempting to allot to each of these three virtues one of the schools of psychotherapy that have emerged from the Viennese soil. The virtue that fits Freudian psychoanalysis is objectivity. Frankl goes on to elucidate with poetic fervor:

> What else could it have been that enabled Sigmund Freud, like Oedipus, to look into the eyes of the Sphinx–the human psyche–and to draw out its riddle at the risk of a most dreadful discovery? In his time such an undertaking was colossal, and so was his accomplishment. Up to then psychology, particularly so-called academic psychology, had shunned everything that Freud then made the focus of his teaching. As the anatomist Julius Tandler jokingly called the 'somatology' which was taught in Vienna's junior high schools 'anatomy with the exclusion of the genital,' likewise Freud could have said that academic psychology was psychology with the exclusion of the libidinal (Frankl, 1985, UG, p. 19).

Frankl continues by pointing out that psychoanalysis not only adopted objectivity–it succumbed to it. Objectivity eventually led to objectivation and reification. He asks, "How it is that psychoanalysis arrived at this technically minded, mechanistic view?" He continues, "This is understandable, considering the intellectual climate in which psychoanalysis emerged, but it must also be understood in the context of the social milieu of the time–a milieu full of prudery. It was a response–a reaction, to be sure, which is 'reactionary,' in that today it is out of date in many respects. But Freud not only reacted to his time, he also acted out of his time" (Frankl, 1985, UG, 19-20).

It is, therefore, not surprising that Freud reached the conclusions he did regarding the *will to pleasure* as a motivation for living upon which the first Viennese school of psychotherapy was founded. Only Freud's later mature works, *Beyond the Pleasure Principle* (1920), *The Future of an Illusion* (1927), and *Civilization and its Discontents* (1930) entertain the wider spectrum of influences beyond the repression of sexuality and its attendant pathology.

Freud's professional lineage was continued through the influence he had on his colleagues, even though some of them later went on to found their own systems of psychotherapy, most notably, Alfred Adler and Carl G. Jung. Although having studied in Vienna and being close by geographic proximity, Jung, in Switzerland, was not in direct line of the Viennese schools of psychotherapy; therefore, he will not be considered further here. (For more on Jung, see Chapter IX.) Instead, the focus will be on Alfred Adler, whose life and work overlapped that of Freud and had a profound impact on Frankl. Coming back to Schnitzler's list of virtues, Frankl attributes the virtue of "courage" to Adler, stating:

> It is obvious that the virtue of courage fits Adlerian psychology. The Adlerian, after all, regards his entire therapeu-

> tic procedure, in the final analysis, as nothing but an attempt at encouraging the patient. The purpose of this encouragement is to help the patient overcome his inferiority feelings, which Adlerian psychology considers to be a decisive pathogenic factor (Frankl, 1985, UG, p. 23).

It is noteworthy to point out that the Viennese schools of psychotherapy are extensions of each other, each an outgrowth of the preceding system. One builds upon the other. There is continuity, but the focus shifts. This is particularly noticeable when we look at the Freudian and Adlerian systems. The premise that the human being is psychodynamically driven remains the same, only for one it is the *will to pleasure*, and for the other it is the *will to power* that provides the motivation. In view of their Zeitgeist or time gestalt, this is not surprising. Where Freud encountered patients with Victorian attitudes of prudery and tradition-bound values, Adler primarily dealt with patients who had experienced the loss of traditional values and life styles. Following the collapse of the monarchy and being the vanquished of WW-I they felt disempowered and insecure; they were searching for an identity, individually and collectively. They had witnessed a rapid break-down of everything they thought was stable and secure. Their anxieties and fears wore a different mask than their Victorian progenitors had worn. The focus of their search was different from the previous generation's. Adler was able to respond to their needs through his Individual Psychology.

Viktor Frankl (1905-1997)

The young Viktor Frankl in his early years as a medical student at the University of Vienna felt very drawn to Adlerian psychology; he studied under Adler and was even considered his star pupil. His article, "Psychotherapy and the World View," published in Adler's *Journal of Individual Psychology*, in 1925 (when Frankl was only twenty years old) already had a theme that would run through all of his work. "...it concerns *the border area that lies between psychotherapy and philosophy, with special attention to the problems of meanings and values in psychology*" (Frankl, 1997, 59 - 60).

Frankl continued to develop his ideas and came into conflict with Adler. At a session of the Society for Individual Psychology Adler was openly challenged. Adler turned to Frankl and asked him to publicly express his views on the challenge that Adler had received. Frankl tried to present a compromise position that would allow for individual differences and to maintain a dialogue between Adler and his critics. However, Adler would have none of it, and shortly thereafter Frankl was expelled from the society at Adler's insistence (Frankl, 1997, p. 63-64).

Another Viennese compatriot, Joseph Fabry, relates how the young medical student became increasingly dissatisfied with the narrowness of the psychiatric orientation around him. He observed how Freud's ideas, like so many great ideas, had begun to harden into rigid concepts. In Frankl's opinion, what was needed was to understand the human being in his or her totality. "At that point," he recalled later, "I suspended what I had learned from my great teachers and began listening to what my patients were telling me–trying to learn from them" (Fabry, 1987, p. 8). Frankl found many opportunities to listen to patients. After receiving his M.D. degree in 1930, he worked at the neuropsychiatric clinic of the University of Vienna. In addition to his work at the university, Frankl founded "Youth in Distress" counseling centers. Here the fundamental formulations of Existential Analysis (to distinguish it from Freud's Psychoanalysis) and Logotherapy took shape: Frankl's theory postulates that all reality has meaning (*logos*) and that life never ceases to have meaning for anyone; that meaning is very specific and changes from person to person and for each person from moment to moment; that each person is unique and each life contains a series of unique demands that have to be discovered and responded to; that the response to these life demands provides meaning; that happiness, contentment, peace of mind, and self-actualization are mere side products in the search for meaning; and, that the *will to meaning* provides motivation for living (Fabry, 1987, 8-9).

The poet Schnitzler's third virtue, "a sense of responsibility," could be assigned to the third Viennese school of psychotherapy, Viktor Frankl's Existential Analysis and Logotherapy. Its very orientation and motivation, the *will to meaning*, is based on a sense of responsibility. Frank himself thought so when he wrote:

> Just as we could apply the virtue of objectivity to psychoanalysis and that of courage to Adlerian psychology, so it is apt to apply to existential analysis [and logotherapy] the virtue of responsibility. In fact, existential analysis interprets human existence, and indeed being human, ultimately in terms of being responsible. (Frank, 1985, p. 23).

To bring a person to an awareness of his responsibility is the very essence of Franklian theory. Through his Existential Analysis and Logotherapy it is not drives and instincts that come to conscious awareness, but the human spirit with its will to meaning, which seeks to live responsibly (Frankl, 1985, UG p. 23). Existential Analysis is concerned with the present, the "here and now" of existence. From the vantage point of the present it seeks to orient the patient or client to the future where meaning possibilities—waiting to be realized—are stored. Logotherapy, as a treatment modality, provides the means to help a person live his awareness of responsibility.

This opening chapter has given a brief historical overview of the birthplace of psychotherapy. It sketched the culture and the prevailing spirit of the times in Vienna from the turn of the century into the nineteen thirties and beyond. It paralleled historic currents with corresponding psychotherapeutic theories. In broad strokes, it has delineated the progressive development of the Viennese schools of psychotherapy: Freud's, *Psychoanalysis* and Adler's *Individual Psychology*. From this background the next movement in Viennese psychotherapy, Frankl's *Existential Analysis* and *Logotherapy* will be explored at greater depth in subsequent chapters.

VIENNESE SCHOOLS OF PSYCHOTHERAPY

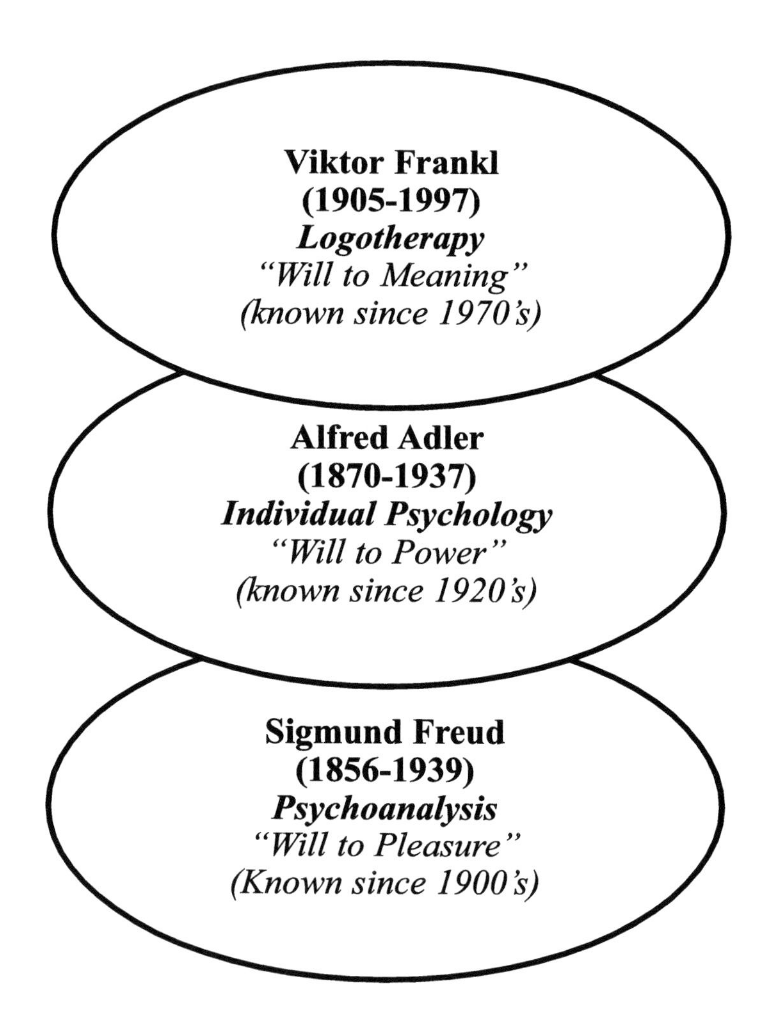

Fig. 1

Viktor Frankl's ***Logotherapy*** has been called the "Third Viennese School of Psychotherapy." It was preceded by Sigmund Freud's ***Psychoanalysis***, and Alfred Adler's ***Individual Psychology***, as the "First" and "Second Viennese School of Psychotherapy," respectively.

Viktor E. Frankl - Biographical Sketch

Born: March 26, 1905; died: September 2, 1997.
Academic titles: M.D. (1930), Ph.D. (1949), Dr.h.c.mult.
Viktor Emil Frankl, M.D., Ph.D., was Professor of Neurology and Psychiatry at the University of Vienna Medical School.
Founder of Logotherapy and Existential Analysis, known as the "Third Viennese School of Psychotherapy."
1940-42 Frankl was director of the Neurological Department of the Rothschild Hospital.
During World War II he spent 3 years at Auschwitz, Dachau and other concentration camps.
From 1946-70 he was director of the Vienna Neurological Policlinic.

A guest professor at several universities in the United States, Frankl has given lectures at 209 universities on five continents. He has received 29 honorary doctorates from universities in all parts of the world and numerous awards in different countries.

Viktor Frankl has authored 32 books which were published in 29 languages. His book *Man's Search for Meaning* has sold over five million copies in the USA alone. According to a survey conducted by the Library of Congress and the Bookof-the-Month Club it belongs to "the ten most influential books in America." (New York Times, November 20, 1991). His last two books *Viktor Frankl–Recollections* and *Man's Search for Ultimate Meaning* were both published in 1997.

The American Medical Society, the American Psychiatric Association and the American Psychological Association have officially recognized Dr. Frankl's Logotherapy as one of the scientifically based schools of psychotherapy. According to the American Journal of Psychiatry, his work is "perhaps the most significant thinking since Freud and Adler."

A detailed Chronology and Extensive Curriculum Vitae of Viktor E. Frankl, M.D., Ph.D., can be viewed at the Official Website of the Viktor Frankl Institute Vienna:

http://www.logotherapy.univie.ac.at or ***http://www.viktorfrankl.org***

II

PHILOSOPHICAL ROOTS of FRANKLIAN THEORIES

Educational and Cultural Influences

Viktor Frankl's innate love of learning was strongly supported by his middle class Jewish family, as well as by the cultural environment of his time and place. In addition to medicine, Viktor Frankl had an avid interest in philosophy, which led him to complete a Ph.D. in Philosophy in 1949, after having earned his M.D. degree, in 1930, at the University of Vienna.

Young Viktor attended Austrian public schools, which are among the best in Europe (according to the *Reader's Digest's Great World Atlas*, 1997, Austria boasts an adult literacy rate of 99%). This, no doubt, is the result of the visionary forethought of the Habsburg Emperor Josef II who mandated public education of all children in 1790. His decrees promoting literacy among all citizens were eagerly carried out. Particularly in Vienna, education has been valued and has had a long history. This becomes evident when one notes the date of the founding of the University of Vienna: 1368.

In Austria, public education beyond the fifth grade is delivered in three tiers, according to student ability. Young people are educated to make their contributions to society through preparation for (a) professional; (b) para-professional; and, (c) vocational fields. Arguably this produces a stratification of society; nevertheless, it also fosters striving for excellence within respective fields of endeavor. As a graduate of the gymnasium (the preparatory track for the professions) and later the university, Viktor Frankl's educational experiences, according to Gould in *Frankl: Life with Meaning*, included: (1) the classical education of the Austrian gymnasium, especially in Greek philosophy and the Aufklärung (German Enlightenment); (2) a medical training dominated by the changes in physical science, especially in psychology; (3) an appreciation of German romanticism; and, (4) a growing awareness of the role of existentialism and phenomenology. Gould goes on to say that two key factors dominated Frankl's education:

> ...liberal Judaism and the humanistic curriculum prescribed by the Austrian state. Free-thinking Judaism liberated him from religious form and dogma. It affirmed a strong social morality, was realistic in the way it viewed life, encouraged an ironic sense of humor, and was marked by what has been described as a mature eroticism. The humanistically oriented state curriculum, designed for the gentile student, provided analyses of the philosophy, literature, history, and science of the Western world. The Renaissance concept of education dominated the course of study, and the humanities were considered the best preparation for the sciences... Although the curriculum was Germanic in spirit and content, it was grounded in Greek classical philosophy (Gould, 1993, p. 27).

Greek Philosophy

From the foregoing description of Frankl's classical education, we can conclude that Frankl was thoroughly familiar with the Greek philosophers and their teachings. Among them was ***Socrates*** (469 - 399 BCE), one of the most original, influential, and controversial figures in ancient Greece. The Athenian, who represents the early philosophical speculations of the Greeks, had the greatest impact in history on Western thought. He redirected the focus of philosophy from considerations about the origin of the universe to what he considered the most important things: developing moral character, and the search for knowledge that would lead to justice. Socrates is credited with the saying "the unexamined life is not worth living" (Huffman, "Socrates," 2001).

Frankl's warm regard for Socrates is evident in the play he wrote, *Synchronization in Birkenwald*, where he casts Socrates in the role of the compassionate advocate for humanity. Socrates is portrayed as the unassuming, patient, elder member among the philosophers who are synchronizing polarities of good and evil, love and hate, time and space through transformative influences to bring about meaningful change in the world. In Frankl's self-revealing dramatic play, philosophers play key roles in their attempt to assist humankind through their wisdom, implying that they have done so since time immemorial (Frankl, 1945, 1-43). Frankl's entire play portrays such familiarity with philosophers and their philosophies, as if he came from their ranks. Like Socrates, he maintains that we learn from the past and look to the future with hope—while living in the present.

Plato (427? - 347? BCE) further developed and revised Greek philosophy. According to Plato, the real nature of any individual thing depends on the form in which it participates. Plato's political philosophy, like his ethics, was based on his theory of the human soul. He argued for the tripartite human soul: (1) the rational part, or intellect; (2) the spirited part, or will; and, (3) appetite or desire. Generally best known for his philosophical idealism, Plato also recognized the importance of the body and emotions, and strove to deal with the whole person in arriving at his understanding of the human soul (Soll, "Plato," 2001).

There are echoes of this in Frankl's logotherapy as will be seen later. Plato's description of the ideal state or society in his *Republic* with its three types of citizens, is analogous to the well functioning soul. Frankl certainly would have been familiar with Plato's metaphysics. He enjoyed using metaphors and analogies, often borrowed from Plato's *Republic* and other works, to illustrate a point.

Where Frankl differs vastly from Plato is in how he views creativity. Plato was critical of art and artists. Plato urged strict censorship of the arts because of their influence on molding people's characters. Since poets and artists usually could not explain their works, Plato thought they were seized by irrational inspiration, a sort of "divine madness" (Soll, "Plato," 2001). By contrast, Frankl greatly encouraged creativity in every form and assigned a high meaning value to creative expression. Frankl saw creativity as an avenue to finding meaning in life, and leading to fulfillment in a unique way.

Aristotle (384 - 322 BCE), may be missing titanic fire, according to Bertrand Russell in *A History of Western Philosophy* (1945), but introduces a fundamental adherence to common sense that Plato often lacks (p. 162). When considering Aristotelean influence on Franklian theories, the pragmatism found in logotherapy comes to mind. Frankl not only encourages philosophizing, but demands that insights gained through such reflection be applied to daily living. Frankl links practical reason with the spiritual dimension to enrich our understanding of truth and wisdom. In the manner of Aristotle, Frankl combines common sense, realistic optimism, moderation, and empirical testing of moral and spiritual values. "Like Aristotle, Frankl employs the Greek *noös* (mind) to include everything that is human and to provide a holistic understanding that avoids the unfocused mysticism of Plato," says Gould (1993, p. 32).

If Aristotle's concern was for civic relationships in his Greek city state, Frankl's concern was for "medical ministry"–reaching out to *homo patiens,* the suffering person. (Frankl, 1970, WM, pp. 116-117). Aristotle's particular charge was to educate Alexander the Great for his future responsibilities to others as a ruler (Soll, "Aristotle," 2000). Frankl showed a similar stand on responsibility in a letter to President Clinton, written by Joe Fabry, quoting Frankl:

> 'The torch [of the Statue of Liberty] that directs 'the poor and huddled masses' toward freedom must be reinforced by an inner light that directs them toward meaningful use of liberty–or the land of the free may become the land of the frustrated.'

Fabry went on to reiterate Frankl's suggestion, made at a World Congress of Logotherapy, that a Statue of Responsibility be erected on the West Coast to balance the Statue of Liberty on the East Coast as a foundation for the future of America (IFL, 1993, Vol. I, p. 42).

The theme of responsibility, like a leitmotiv, runs through Frankl's writings consistently–from responsibility for carrying out the duties that various roles in life impose upon us, to responsibleness, that inner mandate of what I *ought* to do beyond the more obvious what I *should* do.

Aufklärung (German Enlightenment)

Having looked at the influence Greek philosophy has had on Frankl, the next influence to be turned to is the classical humanism of the Aufklärung. According to Gould, "The Aufklärung built strongly on the Greek aphorism, '*know thyself*,' integrating it with the philosophical, psychological, and sociological developments of the late 18th and early 19th centuries." Along these lines of thought, Frankl would have reexamined the role of philosophy and psychology in understanding the nature of human conscience. Although the Aufklärung featured several prominent writers (Christian Thomasius, Christian Wolff, Alexander Baumgarten), its philosophical capstone was ***Immanuel Kant*** (1724 - 1804). (Gould, 1993, 33-34).

In his chief work, *Critique of Pure Reason*, Kant discussed the nature and limits of human knowledge. Kant believed that we cannot justify claims beyond our actual experience as long as we continue to think of the mind and its objects as separate things. He held instead that the mind is actively involved in the objects it experiences. That is, it organizes experience into categories, or forms of understanding. All things capable of being experienced are also arranged in these categories (Jesseph, "Kant," 2001).

Kant's ethical question of "What ought I to do?" reverberates through Frankl's logotherapy. This categorical imperative cannot be avoided. It is a command that comes from within. The categorical imperative of logotherapy is stated as: "Live as if you were living already for the second time and as if you had acted the first time as wrongly as you are about to act now!" (Frankl, 1959, MSFM, p. 132). Another strong parallel we find in Kant and Frankl is that of balancing freedom with responsibleness (exemplified by Frankl's urging that the Statue of Liberty be balanced by a Statue of Responsibility). Accountability is a prominent theme in Kant's ethics, aptly stated as "*ought* implies a *can*" (Gould, 1993, 38-39). Frankl comes close to Kantian accountability by what he calls "the demand quality of life," where life is the questioner and the human person is called to respond to life in the most meaningful way (Frankl, 1970, WM, p. 62).

One of the most influential German philosophers of the Enlightenment era was ***Georg Wilhelm Friedrich Hegel*** (1770-1831). The existential vision of the human person has its foundation in the work of Hegel, titled *Phenomenology of Spirit* (1807). In this work, Hegel describes two primary components that constitute a human person. The first is a biological component. Human beings have a natural, animal dimension. The needs and drives of the biological aspects of humans are similar to those of other animals. The second component of the human being is consciousness and it is this element that distinguishes humans from animals. Consciousness allows humans to transcend the animalistic nature of immediate needs and instincts. Consciousness also gives humans the ability to reflect on and evaluate human life. It permits the formulation of values and a vision of the future, which, in turn, means that humans are able to reflect on their lives and the sum total of their lives' significance. In so doing, humans transcend the limits of their biology (Guignon & Pereboom, 1995, p. xvii - xviii). The theme of self-transcendence also runs strongly through Frankl's logotherapy. In his *Will to Meaning* one reads, "Self-transcendence is the essence of existence" (Frankl, 1970, WM, p. 50).

The concept of alienation, further developed by existentialist writers later, was also based on the writings of Hegel. It is used to describe a sense of separation from nature and a sense of powerlessness in society. It includes a depersonalization of the individual resulting in a loss of personal identity and reality. The individual feels as though life is out of control and that he/she has become the same as an inanimate object (Cooper, 1990, p. 26). Here one is strongly reminded of Frankl's emphatic stand against *reification* and *depersonalization*, of becoming an object instead of a subject (Frankl, 1985, PE, 71-72).

Hegel's view was that all of reality is composed of one Absolute reality, which he termed *Geist*, meaning mind or spirit. Everything that exists is part of a single reality which forms the natural state of unity and wholeness. Alienation begins when the individual thinks of self as being separate from nature, or the natural state of unity and wholeness. In opposing nature, the individual also becomes separate or estranged from self, because the self is part of the whole. This state of alienation is unhappy, wretched, and full of misunderstanding. All of human activity, civilization and history, are seen as attempts to reestablish the lost sense of unity with nature. The goal of *Geist* is self-knowledge and the means of attaining this end is self-reflection. Humans become alienated because of their need to understand themselves as part of the whole. It is only by objectifying reality and viewing it as outside of themselves that humans attempt to understand reality and know their true identity as part of the whole (Cooper, 1990, p.28).

Viktor Frankl's drama, *Synchronization in Birkenwald* implies the same. In the mythic forest of "Birkenwald" forces of light and darkness are at work synchronizing time and space. Awareness of the greater meaning of events, totally incomprehensible in the present, emerges. A timeless unity of events in time and space is revealed and life events are understood in light of this process. In the notes to the play Frankl describes how in 1945, shortly after his release following nearly three years in Nazi prison camps, he wrote *Synchronization in Birkenwald.* He recalls, "It was as if something deep inside me dictated the play. I could hardly write fast enough, even though I used shorthand. The play was written in a few hours" (Frankl, 1945, p. 43).

Existentialism

Existentialism was largely a revolt against traditional European philosophy (according to Ivan Soll, Ph.D., Professor of Philosophy at the University of Wisconsin, Madison), which reached its climax during the late 1700s and early 1800s in the impressive systems of the German philosophers, Immanuel Kant and Georg Wilhelm Friedrich Hegel. Traditional philosophers, Kant and Hegel among them, tended to consider philosophy as a science. They tried to produce principles of knowledge that would be objective, universally true, and certain. The existentialists rejected the methods and ideals of science as being improper for philosophy. They argued that objective, universal, and certain knowledge is an unattainable ideal. They also believed this ideal had blinded philosophers to the basic features of human existence. The existentialists did not make the traditional attempt to grasp the ultimate nature of the world in abstract systems of thought. Instead, they investigated what it was like to be an *individual* human being living in the world. They emphasized the fact that every individual, even the philosopher or scientist seeking absolute knowledge, is only a limited human being. Thus, every person must face important and difficult decisions with only limited knowledge and time in which to make these decisions.

For the existentialists, this predicament lies at the heart of the human condition. They see human life as being basically a series of decisions that must be made, with no way of knowing conclusively what the correct choices are. The individual must continually decide what is true and what is false; what is right and what is wrong; which beliefs to accept and which to reject; what to do and what not to do. Yet, there are no objective standards or rules to which a person can turn for answers to problems of choice, because different standards supply conflicting advice. The individual therefore must decide which standards to accept and which ones to reject (Soll, "Existentialism," 2001). Frankl speaks to this in *Psychotherapy and Existentialism* and points out that logotherapy exceeds and surpasses this ontoanalysis. Logotherapy is concerned with not only *ontos* but also *logos*. In other words, logotherapy is not only analysis but also therapy (Frankl, 1985, PE, p. 17).

The existentialists conclude, therefore, that human choice is *subjective*, because individuals finally must make their own choices without help from such external standards as laws, ethical rules, or traditions. Because individuals make their own choices, they are *free*; but because they freely choose, they are completely *responsible* for their choices. The existentialists emphasize that freedom is necessarily accompanied by responsibility. Furthermore, since individuals are forced to choose for themselves, they have their freedom, and therefore their responsibility, thrust upon them. They are "condemned to be free." They insist that individuals must accept full responsibility for their behavior, no matter how difficult. If an individual is to live meaningfully and *authentically*, he or she must become fully aware of the true character of the human situation and bravely accept it. Authenticity refers to all that a person could be through the active use of his or her powers of awareness and decision making, but has not yet become (Soll, "Existentialism," 2001).

Frankl's logotherapy calls us to live authentically by exercising our freedom of choice in the most meaning oriented way. Frankl addresses the issue of freedom and responsibility in that existentialist vein by stating, "Once meaning orientation turns into meaning confrontation, that stage of maturation and development is reached in which freedom—that concept so much emphasized by the existential philosophy—becomes responsibleness" (Frankl, 1985, PE p. 27).

Existentialism grew out of the work of two notable thinkers of the 1800s: ***Søren Kierkegaard*** (1813 - 1855), a Danish philosopher and Protestant theologian, who is generally considered the founder of the movement; and, ***Friedrich Nietzsche*** (1844 - 1900), a German philosopher. Their emphasis is on the nature of being, existence, through self-knowledge and commitment. The work of Søren Kirkegaard is the first and dramatic example of what Roger Shinn calls the "existentialist posture" (Shinn, 1968, p. 13).

The Socratic *Know thyself*, becomes *Commit thyself* for Kierkegaard and Nietzsche. Ideas without commitment are at best ineffective, and at worst, chimeras that haunt us because we fail to realize them. The lives and works of Kierkegaard and Nietzsche show that commitments can be either theistic or atheistic; but for both men, the key to commitment is the discovery and the use of personal freedom in a pluralist, confusing, and often hostile world. (Gould, 1993, p. 105)

Although Frankl was vehemently opposed to the nihilism or sense of meaninglessness postulated by certain existentialist philosophers, he valued some of their other insights. For instance, on the subject of commitment as an incentive and motivation for living, Frankl often repeated Nietzsche's phrase, "He who has a *why* to live for can bear with almost any *how*" (Frankl, 1985, p. 97). This axiom served him and others well, who had to endure unspeakable hardships. It encouraged them to survive and be reunited with someone who might be waiting for them or to complete a task or a work that was theirs to do.

Beyond Kierkegaard and Nietzsche there are many other thinkers generally considered to be existentialists. Though they often disagree with each other, and sometimes even resent being classified together, they have been grouped together because they share many interests and ideas, and address similar problems. The most prominent existentialist thinkers of the late nineteenth and the twentieth centuries include French writers ***Jean Paul Sartre*** (1905-1980), ***Gabriel Marcel*** (1889-1973), ***Albert Camus*** (1913-1960) and ***Simone de Beauvoir*** (1908-1986); German philosophers ***Karl Jaspers*** (1883-1969), and ***Martin Heidegger*** (1889-1979); Russian religious and political thinker ***Nicolas Berdyaev*** (1874-1948); Jewish philosopher ***Martin Buber*** (1878-1965). Other philosophers whose work is considered to be existentialistic include ***Maurice Merleau-Ponty*** (1908-1961), ***Ortega y Gasset*** (1883-1955), and ***Christopher Rosenzweig*** (1886-1926) (Cooper, 1990, 1-9).

From this impressive list of thinkers in various fields, it can be seen that existentialism was a movement rather than a philosophical system. It attracted not only philosophers, but also journalists, essayists, novelists, and playwrights. It influenced religious, cultural, and political thought; and, it ushered in a new wave of psychology that found expression in the humanistic existential psychotherapies. According to the distinguished psychotherapist Rollo May, "Existentialism is not a system of therapy, but an attitude toward therapy" (May, 1969, p. 15).

Franklian scholar, William Sahakian, elaborates further on the similarities and dissimilarities of logotherapy and existentialism. He emphasizes that logotherapy and French existentialism are equally humanistic, rather than reductionistic; both stress human in place of animalistic qualities. But logotherapy differs from traditional French existentialism in its optimism and panmeaningfulness. Whereas traditional existentialism is pessimistic and stresses the meaninglessness of life, optimistic logotherapy insists that the world is permeated with meaning (Fabry, Bulka, & Sahakian, 1979, p. 58).

Phenomenology

Edmund Husserl, not usually considered an existentialist but the founder of his own movement, *phenomenology*, was nevertheless one of the greatest influences on existentialism. Husserl is the seminal figure in existential phenomenology. The problems that he explored are still challenging contemporary leaders in philosophy and psychology. His aim was: (1) to develop a clear, holistic philosophy of the self; (2) to legitimize philosophically the work of psychology. From these goals he developed a threefold agenda:

1. To establish a method of defining terms and function that will prevent philosophical anarchy.
2. To explain, genetically, how consciousness takes form in human experience.
3. To develop a "pure psychology" of the phenomena of consciousness while avoiding behaviorism.

These challenging goals drew three philosophers into interaction: ***Edmund Husserl*** (1859 - 1938), ***Max Scheler*** (1874 - 1928), and ***Martin Heidegger*** (1889 - 1979); and, led to the establishment of existential phenomenology as a vital force in contemporary thought (Gould, 1993, p. 21- 22).

Heidegger was a pupil of Edmund Husserl who studied under Husserl at the University of Freiburg and, as a result, was profoundly influenced by him. During the nearly forty years by which he outlived his mentor, Heidegger developed his own variation—building on the foundation he had received from Husserl.

Scheler maintained in his "philosophy of the heart" that it is the human heart or the seat of love, rather than a transcendental ego, reason, a will or sensibility, that accounts for the essence of human existence (Frings, "Max Scheler," 2000). This theme certainly runs through Frankl's logotherapy. Sahakian states in

Logotherapy in Action, that "logotherapy is a form of phenomenology," and that the phenomenology to which logotherapy is most closely related is that of Max Scheler (Fabry, et al., 1979, p. 57).

William Blair Gould holds that Husserl, Scheler, and Heidegger, each in his own way, show that an existential, phenomenological approach to life describes how each person experiences the world for himself or herself. The essentials of phenomenology provide a grounding that has proven to be indispensable for the development of existential, philosophical psychology, including *meaning analysis.* Philosophically, phenomenology rethinks Kant's idea of the orderly succession of life to show how individual reason and the phenomena of the world interact. Phenomenology reintroduces Socratic dialogue to help persons use questioning to discover for themselves the meanings of life. It uses the insights of such process philosophers as ***Alfred North Whitehead*** to show how "becoming" is as necessary for understanding life as "being." Phenomenology's concern for the nature of truth established the search for truth as an *a priori* science that uses the transcendental dimension. While attempting to be fully experiential, phenomenology also acknowledges the importance of human intuition as a form of reasoning, which is not strictly rational, but includes an ordering of love in our relationships with others. It teaches that a bracketing of significant occurrences of life can help us to stand back from our problems in order to clarify the essential issues involved (Gould, 1993, p. 101).

Psychologically, phenomenology opposes the traditional, mechanistic, and reductionistic dictates of behaviorism. It also corrects the negative and psychosexual psychotherapy of Freud and his followers. Finally, phenomenology helps us to see that we know ourselves most completely when we understand our being-in-the-world. Both philosophically and psychologically, the perspectives of phenomenology prepared the way for the existential postures that developed, including those of Viktor Frankl (Gould, 1993, p. 101).

Frankl himself defined phenomenology as an attempt to describe the way the human person understands self. It involves the way humans make sense out of their own existence. Phenomenology distances itself from preconceived patterns of interpretation and explanation. Frankl states that the goal of logotherapy, in adopting the method of phenomenological analysis, is to express humanity's objective self-understanding in scientific terms (Frankl, 1969, WTM, p.7).

William Sahakian, Ph.D., D.Sc. (Professor of Philosophy and Psychology, Suffolk University, Boston) offers this summation of "Logotherapy's Place among Philosophies" in *Logotherapy in Action*:

> Logotherapy is a youthful philosophy with an exuberance that conveys an atmosphere of hope. Being a young philosophy, it is undergoing an integration process from which is bound to emerge its ability to cohere with many more facts of human experience. It has the potential to develop into a maturity that could accord it a position among major philosophies. Currently, it offers one of the most adequate answers to the philosophical problems of natural evil such as the existence of human suffering, In this respect logotherapy is a philosophy of religion in addition to being a general philosophy of life (Fabry et al., 1979, p. 58).

Having explored the philosophical roots from which Frankl's logotherapy and existential analysis arose, and having seen the historical framework that surrounded it, we can now focus on logotherapy's attitudes toward religion.

III

LOGOTHERAPY and RELIGION

Franklian Nomenclature

Given the historic framework and the professional climate out of which the Viennese schools of psychotherapy arose, it became necessary to develop a nomenclature that would reflect their differences. The term psychoanalysis designated probing the psychic subconscious and unconscious and did not include the dimension that most deeply inspires man, the noetic or spiritual. Also, psychoanalytic approaches tended to be retrospective, probing a patient's past for hidden drives and repressed material. To contrast his approach from Freud's, Frankl introduced the term ***Existenzanalyse***. *Existenzanalyse* is an assessment of the person within his or her existential paradigm in order to help that person to deal with problems in the most responsible way possible. Existenzanalyse deals with the present, with the "here and now" of situations. As a method of therapy it is less retrospective than psychoanalysis. It focuses instead on the meanings yet to be fulfilled; thereby it becomes a *meaning-centered* psychotherapy. It looks for strengths that could be activated and brought to bear on the existential situation. While acknowledging present difficulties, it looks to the future with hope, trusting that inner resources are available which can be tapped.

When American writers began to publish papers on *Existenzanalyse*, they translated the word as "existential analysis." However, they used the same term to cover the teachings of the late

Swiss psychoanalyst, Ludwig Binswanger who, in the forties, had started to call his teachings *Daseinsanalyse*. Thus *existential analysis* became an ambiguous notion. In order not to add to the confusion, Frankl went back to a term he had coined in the late twenties, ***Logotherapy*** (Frankl, 1967, PE, p.10). In the German literature the term *Existenzanalyse* still prevails, in English the term *Logotherapy* predominates. A fine line of distinction can be drawn: "existential analysis" in the Franklian sense can be thought of as the assessment or diagnostic phase, and "logotherapy" as the treatment phase.

The term *logotherapy* is derived from the Greek words *logos* and *therapy*. The dictionary definition of *logos* is "the controlling principle of the universe" or, in theological terms, "the Word (or Will) of God." Frankl translates *logos* as "meaning." If his translation is accepted, then *meaning* is the controlling principle of the universe; it is at the center of life toward which we all move, consciously or unconsciously (Fabry, 1987, p. 16).

The word *therapy* denotes "treatment," also "having curative or healing properties." It follows, that logotherapy can be interpreted as "treatment or healing through finding meaning." As such, logotherapy focuses on treating/healing the human condition of suffering by finding meaning in human existence; as well as on man's search for such meaning (Frankl, 1985, MSM, p. 121). Frankl admonished his students, when diagnosing pathology, to look through *pathos* at the *logos* which lies beyond it; to look through the suffering at the meaning behind it (Fabry, 1987, p. 21).

"Logotherapy is more than therapy ... it is a view about ourselves and our place in life that will help us make sense of our life in spite of its tragedies," states Fabry in *The Pursuit of Meaning*. He continues, "Logophilosophy puts into a holistic system much of the wisdom of the ages, common sense, and the findings of modern psychology. It can be the basis of self-therapy as well as counseling." (1987, 16-17).

Another key term frequently encountered in Frankl's writings is the Greek noun, *noös*, and the adjectives *noölogical* and *noetic* which are derived from it. *Noös* stands for mind, that aspect of the human person that is specifically human, the human spirit. *Noölogical* and *noetic*, used as qualifiers, refer to the human spirit or to the dimension of the human spirit (Frankl, 1970, WM 17-18). An expanded translation would be: mind that is transcendental, intuitive; inner knowing that is beyond intellectual reasoning and human logic.

Frankl uses the term *noös*, and its derivatives *noölogical* and *noetic*, to include everything that is specifically human, such as: the will to meaning, goal orientation, ideas and ideals, creativity, imagination, faith, love that goes beyond the physical, conscience, self-transcendence, commitments, responsibility, a sense of humor, and the freedom of choice making. The *noös* is that part of us that supplies the resources through which health can be restored and maintained (Fabry, 1987, 18-19).

Please note: For a complete listing of Franklian nomenclature, see "Glossary of Logotherapeutic Terms and Phrases" in the appendix.

Religion and Psychology

Religions—in all their diversity—have attempted to bestow meaning upon the whole of existence. Whether we side with a single tradition, or whether we are ready to open our hearts to the wisdom inherent in all of them, we find that religion has looked at ultimate life questions longer than any other branch of human knowledge. When we allow religion to speak to us, and listen to what it has to teach, we find that it has addressed these essential human questions:

1) Who Am I? Where did I come from? Where am I going?
The first set of questions, which religion attempted to answer, dealt with our origin and our place in the universe. The answers any given religion formulated gave a sense of belonging to its adherents; it fostered security and well-being that comes from being an integral part of something.

2) How do I relate to others: to my Creator and to all of creation?
The second kind of questions dealt with ethics (virtues and vices). Out of these questions came rules that regulated worship and social order. Answers to these questions established moral codes upon which civilizations were built.

3) What is the purpose of life? How do I fulfill my life's mission?
Questions of the third category had to do with vision and direction. If the vision of life's purpose was grand, it resulted in expansion. When it was limiting, it led to contraction. Religion attempted to give guidelines for living in order to attain life's goals and reach for *ultimate meaning.*

Historically most wisdom traditions did not separate philosophy from religion, or psychology from spirituality, but incorporated everything into their philosophy of religion. They challenged their followers to live the ideals espoused by their particular religious understanding—sometimes leading to their glory, at other times to their destruction—depending on their concept of God and their image of man.

The Twentieth Century has been an innovative century in many ways; particularly, in understanding the human person through the new discipline of psychology. In ages past, there had hardly been a division between spirit and psyche because religion dealt with all phases of human awareness. With the exploration into the human psyche by the new behavioral sciences, a silent wall arose between spirituality and psychology. Spirituality was deemed by psychology as belonging to religion, while the emotions and intellect became the purview of psychology. Furthermore, this division was seen as necessary due to the inherently different functions of religion and psychotherapy: Religion is concerned with salvation; psychotherapy is concerned with mental health. Understanding the objectives of religion and psychotherapy is crucial to understanding their different approaches to the self.

While both psychotherapy and religion are concerned, in different ways, with reconciliation and consolation, the aim of psychotherapy is to foster health, and the aim of religion is to help its followers achieve eternal life through liberation from bondage to sin. Frankl points out that though the aims are dissimilar, what happens in each case may be the same. Frankl is quoted as saying: "Although religion may not aim at mental health, it might result in it. Psychotherapy, in turn, often results in an analogous by-product; while the doctor is not, and must not be, concerned with the patient to regain his belief in God, time and again this is just what occurs, unintended and unexpected as it is" (Gould, 1993, p. 60).

Frankl's major statements on religion were first expressed in a book titled *Der Unbewusste Gott* in 1947. (In 1975, he authorized an English translation, which appeared under the title *The Unconscious God.*) Since that first venture in this direction, the relationship of religion to psychotherapy was further explored and propounded by Frankl in lectures, articles, and books during the next fifty years of his long life. His views on religion and religion's place in psychotherapy are best summarized in his 32nd and last book, *Man's Search for Ultimate Meaning* (1997), where he equates the search for God with man's search for Ultimate Meaning.

Frankl's Position on Religion

Frankl was a devout, though liberal Jew. As stated earlier, free-thinking Judaism liberated him from religious form and dogma. Only a deeply religious man, a man of faith, would say, "It is my contention that faith in the ultimate meaning is preceded by trust in an ultimate being, by trust in God." (1970, WM, p. 145). He speaks of religion's inestimable contribution to mental health stating, "After all, religion provides man with a spiritual anchor, with a security such as he can find nowhere else." (1970, WM, p. 144)

When Frankl was asked if there was a trend away from religion, he pointed out that in his observation the trend was not away from religion, but away from the emphasis on the differences between individual denominations. No, he did not foresee a sort of universal religion, rather the contrary. He foresaw a trend toward a profoundly personalized religion, where every person will arrive at a language of his or her own, of finding uniquely personal ways to communicate with the Ultimate Being (1970, WM, p. 154).

On another occasion Frankl offered the following analogy in answer to the "Where is God?" question: A youngster is planting his tripod on solid ground in order to mount his telescope, so he can look at the heavens and find the planets. At first he is excited by all that he sees. After a while, he gets frustrated because he cannot find what he wants to see the most through his telescope, namely, the planet Earth. He wants to know why it is hidden from his view when everything else is plainly visible. Only when he is asked where his tripod is planted does it begin to dawn upon him that the Earth is too close to be seen "out there." So it is with God.

Frankl was careful in his work to differentiate his views on psychology and religion. He gives the following explanation why he so adamantly kept religion and psychotherapy separate and distinct:

> Fusion of psychotherapy and religion necessarily results in confusion, for such fusion confounds two different dimensions, the dimension of anthropology and theology. As compared with the dimension of anthropology, that of theology is the higher one in that it is more inclusive. (1970, WM, p. 144)

Frankl believed logotherapy to be a philosophy of life, a personality theory and a school of psychology with specific methods and techniques. As a philosophy of life, he believed that logotherapy was universally applicable. He also believed his personal faith to be just that, personal. He drew boundaries between psychology and theology and described the difference as being "the healing of the soul and the salvation of the soul." In some of Frankl's final works, he did write about what he called "pure coincidence" and reflected on "whether behind an apparent coincidence a higher, or deeper, ultimate meaning may be hidden" (Frankl, 1997, p. 57).

While Frankl wrote of concepts that are clearly theistic, he continued to differentiate between logotherapy, as a philosophy of life, and theology. Philosophy is the love and pursuit of truth. Theology is the study of religious questions and phenomena. Theological thought contains faith in Divine revelation as a presupposition. It usually includes the traditions of a particular religion and claims regarding religious truth and dogma, as well as the explanation of various mysteries that cannot be rationally justified; and, it is concerned with religious rituals.

Given his persistent striving to keep religion distinct from psychology, Frankl disliked many of the terms used in the English translation of his works from German. The English words "soul" and "spirit" have strong connotations of definite religious significance. In German, the original words "Seele" and "Geist" do not have the corresponding inference of a religious connotation. For example, the German title of his major work, *Ärztliche Seelsorge*, in the English translation became *The Doctor and the Soul.* This is unfortunate because the German title closer approximates "Medical Ministry." Frankl was well aware of the dedication inscribed above the General Hospital in Vienna that houses most of the university clinics: "Saluti et solatio aegrorum–to the Care and Consolation of the Sick." Frankl quotes the prophet Isaiah in that context, stating, "I, for one, believe that the words, 'Comfort ye, comfort ye my people' (Isaiah 40:1) are as valid [today] as when they were written and are also addressed to the doctors among 'his people.' This is the way every good doctor has understood his responsibility all along." (1970, WM, p. 125). That was the intention of his work, *Ärztliche Seelsorge* (*The Doctor and the Soul*), which is considered his magnum opus. It is the most systematically structured work, outlining his theory of psychotherapy from existential analysis to logotherapy; its methods and techniques, as applicable from general problem areas of life to special areas of pathology.

Frankl feared that the title of his major work, translated as *The Doctor and the Soul* worked as a deterrent, at least in the eyes of scientifically minded psychiatrists and psychologists. And that the book, which outlined the theoretical framework of a new approach to psychotherapy, due to its title, would be relegated to "inspirational reading," instead of being seen as a serious professional contribution (Frankl, 1955, DS, p. xii). This was particularly disturbing to him because, he felt, he had followed the professional code and had more sharply delineated the distinction between religion and psychology more than any other professional. Given the spirit of the times, this may have been necessary. One wonders if half a century later this would still be the case?

Frankl was a psychiatrist and recognized his obligation as a medical doctor and a scientist to maintain the development of logotherapy as a scientific theory that is universally applicable. At the same time, Frankl brought his scientific skills to bear on the dimension of the human person that has traditionally been reserved to religion. Frankl defined religion generally as the expression of the quality within the human being that searches for ultimate meaning. Logotherapy is a meaning-centered psychotherapy that considers the meaning-seeking quality of humans to be a facet of human nature, and considers the psychological aspects of this human characteristic. Logotherapy is not concerned with religious belief or doctrine, only the characteristics of humans that make a search for meaning (that is frequently found in religious expression) a significant aspect of the human being (Pascoe, 1995, 72-73).

☙

Although Frankl tried very hard to stay on the scientific side of the fence that divides psychology and religion, John Morgan in *From Freud to Frankl: Our Modern Search for Personal Meaning* points out, "That Frankl's psychology and Jewish philosophy are intertwined is indisputable" (Morgan, 1987, p. 157). And, it is none other than Rabbi Harold Kushner, who wrote the endorsement for Viktor Frankl's last work, stating: "One of the great souls of our time shares with us the distilled wisdom of a lifetime of personal and professional experience in *Man's Search for Ultimate Meaning*" (Kushner, 1997, MSUM, frontice piece).

Logotherapy's Attitude Toward Religion

Believing religious faith to be a human phenomenon, Frankl felt that as such it must be taken seriously from a psychological perspective. Taking a serious approach to religion allows the therapist to utilize the spiritual resources of the person. Spiritual is defined in this instance as being a unique and truly human aspect of human beings, and therefore an authentic area of concern for a therapist (Frankl, 1969, WTM, p. 140). This is the attitude we see reflected in his logotherapy.

Frankl related the religious dimension of the human person to the human capacity to use symbols. Language is a system of symbols. In a like sense, religion is also a system of symbols (Frankl, 1969, WTM, p. 153). Frankl stated that in the final analysis each person encounters his/her deity alone and religion symbolizes this fact of human existence. There is a human tendency for individuals, who experience God in a particular way, to group together. Various religious denominations are groups of people that utilize religious symbols in a common way. This is similar to the human use of language and the fact that various languages exist and yet many share the same alphabet (Frankl, 1969, WTM, p. 155). The scientific study of human religious symbology and how an individual's use of religious symbols can contribute to psychological health is a legitimate area for psychological investigation (Pasco, 1995, 116-117).

Frankl discussed the dimensional difference between psychotherapy and religion in terms of anthropology and theology. He does this by comparing the human world to the world of the animal. The human person has a level of comprehension of the characteristics and abilities inherent in animal life. However, an animal cannot comprehend the human world. Frankl stated, "...the ratio between man and the animal is somewhat similar to the ratio between God and man." (Frankl, 1969, WTM, p. 144). Frankl used the following example to illustrate this point: "...an ape that is being used to develop poliomyelitis serum, and for this reason is punctured again and again, is not able to grasp the meaning of its suffering, for with its limited intelligence it cannot enter into the world of man, the only world in which its suffering is understandable. Is it not conceivable that there is still another dimension possible, a world beyond man's world, a world in which the question of an ultimate meaning of human suffering will find an answer?" (Frankl, 1969, WTM, p. 145).

Logotherapy, as a scientific discipline dealing with philosophy and techniques of treatment, Frankl believed, should be available to every person and utilizable by any therapist. It is irrelevant whether the individual person or therapist's persuasion is theistic, agnostic or atheistic (Frankl, 1969, WTM, p. 143).

Logotherapy's Compatibility with Religion

During the Jubilee Congress in Vienna, in 1995, held to celebrate Viktor Frankl's 90th birthday, logotherapy's appeal to the religious world was obvious. The roster of key speakers and presenters at that glittering conference included many theologians (Seidel, 1996, 5-7). The appeal of logotherapy was further mirrored in the audience of 1,200 participants. Many of the participants wore religious garb or displayed insignia, indicative of various religious persuasions and faith traditions.

Robert Leslie, Ph.D., Professor Emeritus of Pastoral Psychology and Counseling at the Pacific School of Religion, states that Viktor Frankl's logotherapy has received a positive appraisal from the religious world almost from the beginning. He cites four major reasons why the religious world embraces logotherapy:

1) Logotherapy gives a central place to religious values and the principle of transcendence. Religious values, if meaningful to a client, can be a major source of strength to be activated to bring about self-transcendence.
2) Logotherapy's holistic—body, psyche, and spirit—approach to psychotherapy gives the therapist the role of looking for and activating clients' strengths, instead of searching for pathology.
3) Logotherapy assigns a positive role to unavoidable suffering and hardships of life. Logotherapy points to the inner freedom to take a stand and activate attitudinal values to deal with suffering.
4) Logotherapists assist clients in their search for meaning, which is unique to each individual. Logotherapy seeks to help a client to discover that meaning and to express it through action. The Judaeo-Christian faith has always insisted on the uniqueness of every person and can support that tenet of logotherapy. (IFL, 1995, Vol. I, pp. 33-35).

Leslie's article includes an appraisal of logotherapy by the prominent psychologist, Gordon Allport, stating, "Gordon Allport believed that history will record that the psychoanalytic era in Europe and America was the time when psychology lost its soul, and that Viktor Frankl was instrumental in helping psychology find its soul again." (p. 35).

☙

In this writer's opinion, there is an even deeper reason for the acceptance of logotherapy by the religious world than the four reasons listed by Dr. Leslie. There is a common ground upon which religion and logotherapy are both standing: **It is spirituality**. Religion may value spirituality for different reasons than logotherapy does, but both recognize that spirituality is the bedrock upon which their systems are built, whether a belief system of a given religion, or a therapeutic system that is concerned with holistic healing.

What is spirituality? Ewert Cousins, general editor of an all-encompassing undertaking, *World Spirituality: An Encyclopedic History of the Religious Quest*, points out that spirituality should be distinguished from theology and the study of religion. The inner dimension of the person is called "the spirit" by certain traditions. He continues, "This spiritual core is the deepest center of the person. It is here that the person is open to a transcendent dimension; it is here that the person experiences ultimate reality" (Cousins, 1983, p.1).

Reflecting on that, one comes to understand that spirituality is an inherent part of being human; it is the essential core of a human being; it is the indwelling spirit of *theos* (Greek: *God*). Theology then becomes the study of that indwelling God/spirit which is the source of our being. It is also the study of our relationship to theos, God personified in theistic religions. Systems of beliefs and rituals have been developed to reach that spirit within, and to enter into communion with God/spirit. We call these systems religions. Religions assist their adherents to reach out to and to experience God, according to their particular understanding. It follows then that spirituality is at the core, innate and central; and, that a particular religion is acquired and peripheral to the core. Frankl's logotherapy addresses that central spiritual core through psychotherapy, not through any particular religious persuasion.

It is extremely important for pastoral psychologists (and all those who have the health and well-being of others at heart) to understand these distinctions between spirituality and religion—especially when working with persons of religious persuasions different than their own. We need to keep in mind that every person has a spiritual core and that there are "many paths to the same summit" (Smith, 1991, p.72). Some paths are religious, some are non-religious; some are theistic in their orientation, some are non-theistic in their understanding of the Source of Being. The therapeutic process will take on a hopeful note when this presupposition that spirituality is central, and the particular religion of a client is incidental, is remembered.

The topic of logotherapy's compatibility with religion is specifically addressed by Dr. Donald F. Tweedie, Jr., Professor Emeritus of Psychology in the Fuller Theological Seminary Graduate School of Psychology. Writing in 1979, he pointed out that one of the thorny problems for the churchman in meeting the call to be a counselor was the general mood of contemporary psychotherapy. The mainstream of clinical counseling, as well as the text and the context of the training facilities, were a secular enterprise. Religious values were avoided and religious genius, in the sense of William James, was regarded as a grave symptom. Tweedie continued:

> Logotherapy seemed a more compatible approach to counseling. It is comfortable with religious terminology and religious goals. The title of Frankl's first theoretical book to be translated into English was *The Doctor and the Soul*. Its original German title, *Aerztliche Seelsorge*, is even more unabashedly religious in tone: 'Medical Ministry' or 'The Medical Care of Souls.' The term logotherapy also struck a responsive note to churchmen. Even those who knew little Greek knew that, 'In the beginning was the *Logos*.'

> The logotherapist sees man as having an essential and primary spiritual dimension. The image of God in man is neither an object of denial nor a victim of reductionism. Instead of being inexorably determined by internal and external forces, man is free. He has the power of contrary choice and is held responsible for his choosing. To understand and cure man's ills, he must be understood in his spirituality with its potentials for transcending his physical and psychological dimensions. These messages from a prominent and articulate scholar-psychiatrist were gladly heard by churchmen (Tweedie, 1979, pp. 144-145).

Based on the observations and evaluations of logotherapy's compatibility with religion by the distinguished pastoral psychologists and educators, Drs. Leslie and Tweedie, one can draw the conclusion that logotherapy is not only compatible with religion, but also emerges as a psychotherapy that has the most to offer to churchmen and -women.

This view was also expressed by Kazimier Popielski, who compared Frankl's concept of human nature with that of Karol Wojtyla, pointing out that both Viktor Frankl and Pope John Paul II place the spiritual dimension, calling for self-transcendence, centrally in their image of the human person (Popielski, 1982, pp. 55-60).

Ecumenical and Cross-Cultural Appeal of Logotherapy

As our planet is circumnavigated by more and more of its inhabitants, due to unprecedented advances in communication and travel, it is inevitable that ideologies will impinge on one another as never before. No longer can we live in isolation and indulge in parochial thinking. It is becoming increasingly obvious that we are moving toward a global civilization, and that will necessitate that we think globally.

Given the diversity of religious beliefs on our shrinking planet, it may be helpful to look to an agency outside of our own faith tradition to act as a bridge that connects us to others. This bridge will have to offer something of value to all people, who share time on this planet. If we look at the world and our fellow human beings and ask what we have in common, instead of what divides us, we find the following: What is central unites us; what is peripheral divides us. Human beings, aside from cultural differences, have individual differences of size and shape, personalities, and belief systems. Yet, inherent in the human condition are factors we have in common. Among them are:

- Our yearning to be connected to the source of life.
- Our need for community with other human beings.
- Our innate longing to experience life as meaningful, even sacred.

Much of the work of pastoral psychology will revolve around these key points and the issues arising from them. In and of themselves they present an ecumenical posture because they cut through differences of religious and cultural idioms. When looking for psychotherapeutic approaches to pastoral psychology, I found two extremes:

1. Therapies that ignored the human spirit entirely.
2. Approaches to pastoral counseling that were *too religious* (entirely faith based; often with heavy denominational bias).

It might be timely here to emphasize what pastoral psychology is NOT: faith healing, Biblical counseling, or a substitute for spiritual direction. It is instead, a science and an art that endeavors to treat afflictions of the human psyche and spirit. As a science it deals with facts; as an art it addresses values. That may well include religious values of the client, but more importantly, it must see the spiritual values of the client.

In order for pastoral psychology to be universally applicable as a professional discipline, it must be ecumenical and not denominationally biased in intent. An analogy from medicine will help illustrate this point: Penicillin works as an antibiotic (where an antibiotic is indicated) regardless of who administers it. If pastoral psychology wishes to establish its credibility as a discipline that can be counted on by all, it must do the same. It will have to be effective as a psychotherapy because it addresses that which is central in the lives of those it treats, regardless of their religious orientation, or the faith tradition of those who administer it.

Therefore, the tools employed to achieve that end will need to be appropriate for the task. Few tools have been designed to date by psychology to reach the innermost core, the aspect pastoral psychology often needs to reach. One notable exception in the arsenal of treatment modalities, which addresses the human spirit in its treatment model, is Viktor Frankl's logotherapy. Not only can logotherapy serve as an excellent tool in the hands of the skilled pastoral psychologist, but it has universal and ecumenical appeal. This is evidenced by its use in many cultures with their respective religious persuasions; also, it speaks to the churched and to the unchurched. Logotherapy appeals to Christians and Jews, Buddhists, Muslims, Hindus, and others. As a matter of fact, logotherapy's primary appeal seems to be to the religious sector. Psychiatry deems logotherapy to be too philosophical, and philosophy accuses it of being too religious. It may well be religious, but in a universal, spirit-centered way.

Logotherapy seeks to find the **logos**–the meaning–that which gives reason for being. As such, it assists pastoral psychologists and all who are working to facilitate psycho-spiritual health to help their clients to look for the highest and noblest; for that which is worthy of their humanity; and, to express it by living their knowing responsibly. That aim has ecumenical and universal appeal because it echoes the intention of every religion and every culture which has sought to help its people become the best they can be!

Common Problems Brought to Pastoral Caregivers

Having examined logotherapy's attitudes toward religion, ascertained its compatibility with religion, and confirmed its ecumenical disposition it becomes evident that logotherapy is theoretically ideally suited as a treatment modality for pastoral psychology. Frankl emphasizes that logotherapy as a scientific discipline–dealing with philosophy and techniques of treatment–should be utilizable by any therapist (Frankl, WTM, 1969, p. 143).

It is pointed out in the *Pastoral Counseling Treatment Planner* (Kok and Jongsma, 1998) that troubled people often turn first to their spiritual advisors for counseling. In fact, research has shown that nearly fifty percent of the population, whether Catholic, Protestant, or Jewish, asked for help from their religious leaders before anyone else. And increasingly, even secular counselors are integrating spirituality into their psychotherapeutic practices (p. 1).

James R. Kok, Director of Care Ministries, The Crystal Cathedral in Garden Grove, California, salutes the pastoral psychologists with this moving paragraph in the preface to the above named work as follows:

> These frontline men and women of ministry hold a prime position of honor and respect in my roster of valued

SYMBOL FOR LOGOTHERAPY

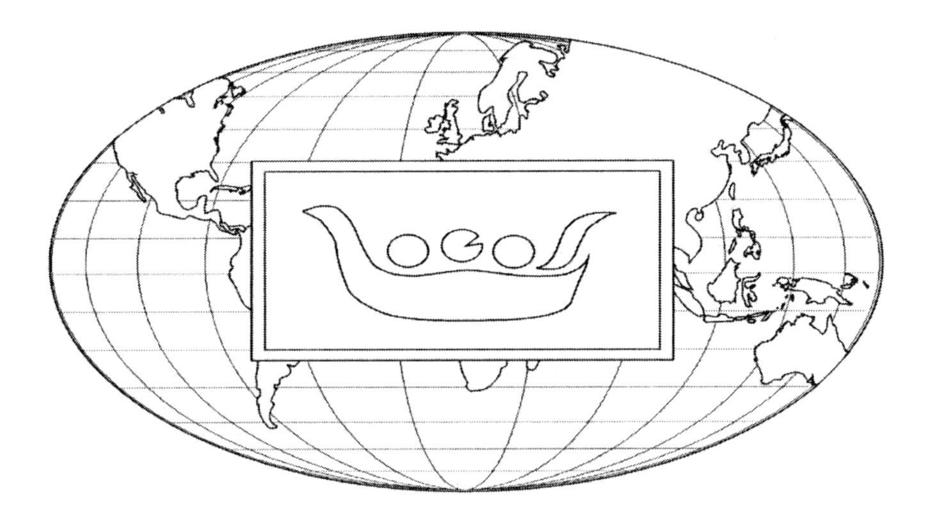

Fig. 2

The above symbol, created by the founder of the Viktor Frankl Institute of Logotherapy in the United States, Joseph Fabry, J.D., attempts to capture essential elements of logotherapy:

The **BOAT** seen above, is the Greek symbol for **wisdom**.

The implied **OIL LAMP** is the Hebrew symbol for **eternity**.

The **GLOBE** stands for Monanthropism, Oneness of Humankind.

L-O-G-O-S is what you are really seeing superimposed on the globe above. Not a boat, not an oil lamp, but *LOGOS*.

In John 1:1 it is written: "*En archa ain ho Logos, kai ho Logos ain tou Theou, kai ho Logos ain Theo.*" Translated: "In the beginning was the Word [*Logos*], and the Word was with God, and the Word was God."

Logos translated as **meaning** brings together, unifies, is central to life.

(Rice, 2002, PowerPoint Presentation; used with permission)

> human beings... To me these pastoral people represent the best of God's good people. Week in and week out, people dealing with a smorgasbord of trials, conflicts, and dysfunctions show up on their doorsteps asking for help. And those people are always welcomed in. Weeping, perplexed, in despair, angry, injured, and ill, they come to the church, cathedral, synagogue, or temple expecting to meet God's servants, and they do (p. vii).

It is only fitting that these "God's servants" be offered the best tools available for aiding them to meet their daily challenges. Viktor Frankl's logotherapy is such a tool because it speaks to life's challenges that are part of the human condition with hope; it treats the "weeping, perplexed, in despair, angry, injured..." who appear at the doors of those who integrate spirituality in their psychotherapy as persons undergoing transformation.

The most common problems brought before pastors, priests, ministers, and rabbis, as well as others dealing in pastoral psychology as counselors, mentors, spiritual directors or advisors are the following (as listed alphabetically in *The Pastoral Counseling Treatment Planner*, pp. v-vi):

Adult Child Disappointment
Aging Parents
Anger Toward God
Chemical Dependence
Child's Medical Condition
Chronic Illness
Death of Child
Death of Spouse
Dependent Adult Child
Depression [Grief]

Divorce
Family Conflict
Financial Crisis
Guilt
Infertility
Interpersonal Hurt
Legal Problems
Loneliness
Marital Conflict
Medical Condition
Mental Illness in Family
Parent-Child Conflict/Adolescence
Prayer Struggles
Premarital Counseling
Religion/Spirituality Differences
Sexual Abuse Victim
Sexual Orientation Conflict
Spiritual Doubts
Suicidal Ideation
Unemployment
Unwanted Pregnancy

If there is anything this pastoral counselor would add to this impressively comprehensive list, it would be "life transition" issues. When we find ourselves displaced in our own life, due to sudden or even expected change, a temporary lack of identity often results. Some transitional phases are well recognized, such as: Starting school, leaving home, job relocation, the "empty-nest" syndrome, retirement, etc. Consider the following examples; how would you—as the sought out helper—respond?

A little girl (age four) has been eagerly preparing to be the "Big Sister" when the expected new baby arrives in the family. She had even attended the Super-Sib (sibling) program offered by the hospital where mother would go to have the baby. There she learned about the needs of newborns and how to be Mommy's little helper after the baby arrived. She had a dolly that needed to be fed and changed to practice with and a certificate to prove that as a graduate of the Super-Sib program she is duly qualified to be a Big Sister.

The shock of her young life came when her eagerly awaited baby brother died shortly after birth. Her entire focus lately had been on preparing to be the Big Sister. She tried hard to comprehend the enormity of what had happened and was torn between loss and confusion. At the funeral she followed the minister around waiting for an opportune moment to ask her burning question. Finally, finding the courage, she tugged at the ministerial robe and earnestly asked, "Rev. Marge, am I still a Big Sister now?" (Told to the author by The Rev. Marjorie Swacker, Disciples of Christ Minister.)

Or consider the case of the dignified older gentleman who faced a different identity crisis. He answered my question, "What brings you to counseling?" in this manner:

"I looked into the mirror and this old man looked back at me. I don't know who he is." As his story unfolded, it became clear that since childhood he had led an extraordinarily busy and successful life. Then, in fairly rapid succession, his wife of many years died, their last child left home and moved far away (as the other children had done). Finding the rambling house, which had been home to his large family too big for his needs, he sold it and moved to a smaller one (only to find that after more than a year there, he had not unpacked his boxes yet).

Continuing to state his reasons for needing to talk to someone, he said, "The last and worst thing that happened was when my accountant urged me to close my office because it was no longer profitable! That was a terrible blow!" This man had been accustomed to the routine of spending his working hours with two valued employees, who had been with him for many years. They had worked well work together in their chosen profession and derived fulfillment from doing meaningful work.

Where this man had previously identified himself as a professional, and through his roles as husband and father, he was at a loss now since that identity was no longer current. Another shock was his realization, "The years have flown by and now I am old. I don't know how to be old."

These are genuine life questions that are being asked. Neither the little girl's, nor the older man's anguish can or should be considered as psychopathology. What does pastoral counseling or any other intervention have to offer them?

As we can see from the common problems listed previously, their range encompasses despondency, despair, doubt, and confusion, those tendencies which Frankl views as the underlying dynamics of most human misery. His logotherapeutic interventions show us how to address the root of the problem, not just the out-pictured phenomenology or the presenting symptom.

Please note: It is not the intention of this treatise, nor is it in the domain of pastoral psychology, to attempt to treat conditions that are the province of psychiatry. Frankl, as a psychiatrist, treated severe mental illness clinically and medically. That part of his work is not to be considered here. Only his philosophy and the application thereof to the trials and tribulations arising from the human condition, which is the legitimate domain of pastoral psychology, will be addressed in this study.

IV

BASIC CONCEPTS of LOGOTHERAPY

Fundamental Tenets of Logotheory

There is a theory—a *theoria*, i.e., a vision, a *Weltanschauung*—underlying the practice of logotherapy, maintains Viktor Frankl in his book, *Psychotherapy and Existentialism* (1985, 17-18). He continues by pointing out that logotherapy is based on three fundamental assumptions that form a chain of interconnected links:

1. Freedom of Will
2. Will to Meaning
3. Meaning of Life

These are the three tenets upon which logotherapy is based. They form the foundation on which Franklian theory rests. It is arguable whether scientific proof for "Freedom of Will" or "Meaning of Life" exists; they must be regarded as virtual axioms. However, the middle tenet, "Will to Meaning," as a primary motivating force of human beings is provable; and, it has been proved through psychological studies. For example, the *Purpose in Life Test* (Crumbaugh & Maholick, 1981) has been used with large populations and has validated Frankl's assumptions (Lukas, 2000, p.5).

Freedom of Will

Freedom of will is the concept that the human being has the capacity of free choice. Humans are finite beings and human freedom is restricted by circumstances. The freedom with which

Frankl is concerned is not freedom from conditions, but the freedom to choose one's attitude toward whatever conditions exist—the freedom to take a stand. Humans are free to choose how a given situation will be regarded, what meaning, or if meaning will be found in the circumstances of life. Frankl asserts that each person is ultimately self-determining. Each person decides what his or her life will be by the choices that are made moment to moment. This gives each individual the freedom to change the direction of his or her life; and, consequently self-determine who one will become (Frankl, 1970, WTM, 16 - 25).

One of the essential qualities of human nature is the ability to rise above, or grow beyond, the conditioning of biological, psychological or sociological factors. This makes human nature essentially unpredictable. By the ability to choose, each person is capable of changing the world for the better. Freedom is always in danger of disintegrating into arbitrariness unless it is lived with responsibility. Frankl maintains that there is no condition, no state of the severest psychosis that can totally rob a human being of freedom, however limited the remaining residue of freedom might be. This is the core dignity of the human being. Referring to his concentration camp experience, Frankl states, "Man *can* preserve a vestige of spiritual freedom, of independence of mind, even in such terrible conditions of psychic and physical stress." (1985, MSM, p. 86).

Will to Meaning

The second of the basic tenets of logotherapy is that finding meaning or the *will to meaning* is the primary motivation for living. This differs from Freud, who postulated that the primary human drive is the *will to pleasure*; and, from Adler, who taught that the *will to power* was the fundamental human motivation (Frankl, 1985, MSM, 121-130).

The meaning that an individual finds is unique and specific to each person and can be fulfilled only by that one person and no one else. Frankl emphasized that the true meaning of each person's life is something that must be discovered by activity in the world through interaction with others; and, not solely through introspection (within the internal psychological makeup of the individual), as if each person were a self-contained system. Challenging a person with a potential meaning to fulfill evokes the will to meaning from a state of latency (Frankl, 1985, MSM, 121-133).

The will to meaning is not considered a "drive" in humans. If that were the case, then it would be in the same category as other drives identified by Freud. It would follow then that people are primarily motivated to maintain inner equilibrium as postulated in the principle of homeostasis. Frankl absolutely opposes this interpretation. Frankl saw a fundamental difference between being driven to attain something, and human striving for attainment of a goal or purpose. The human being is pushed by drives, but is drawn forward by the pursuit of meaning (Frankl, 1969, WTM, p. 43).

In order to fulfill the will to meaning, a person is capable of suffering and coping with the inherent frustrations and stresses of life. In extreme situations, the person is even prepared to voluntarily give up life for the sake of an ideal (p. 167). A strong will to meaning promotes human health, both physically and mentally, and prolongs, as well as preserves, life (p. 48).

The despair that a person feels when unable to find meaning is evidence that the will to meaning exists as a significant component within the person. The fact that individuals have an innate desire to find meaning verifies the existence of meaning in the human life (p. 95). Frankl believed that every crisis was also an opportunity to discover new elements of meaning in the challenge of the situation. He maintained that we have the freedom, within obvious limitations, to fulfill the meaning of our lives (p. 167-168).

Meaning of Life

The third basic tenet of logotherapy teaches that meaning is contained within the concrete experiences of daily life. In addition, each person has a special purpose to fulfill in life. Each person is unique and cannot be replaced by another. There will not be a second chance to fulfill the special assignment for which the individual is responsible in life. The task is specific and unique, as is the opportunity to accomplish the task. Frankl termed it the "the demand quality of life." Each situation in life is a challenge or presents a problem for the individual to solve. It is life that asks questions of the individual and each person must answer by freely choosing to respond to life. Logotherapy sees responsibleness as being the essence of human existence. The meaning of life is always changing, but it never ceases to exist. Life has meaning under all circumstances, even the most challenging ones (1985, MSM, p. 131-133).

Frankl states, "While no logotherapist *prescribes* a meaning he may well *describe* it. This means describing what is going on in a man when he experiences something as meaningful, without applying to such experiences any preconceived pattern of interpretation. In short, our task is to resort to a phenomenological investigation of the immediate data of actual life experience" (Frankl, 1985, PE, 28-29).

These major tenets of logotherapy can be tested by experience. They have been found acceptable by people regardless of beliefs—from Jesuits to Orthodox Jews, atheists and agnostics, by people from East to West. They speak like a perennial philosophy or ancient wisdom that has stood the test of time and make good sense upon reflection. The content of these fundamental tenets of logotherapy can be summarized as follows:

1) We have the freedom of will, within obvious biological and sociological, even psychological limitations, to fulfill the meaning of our lives. By doing so, we determine who we become.
2) The will to meaning is the primary motivation for living. We are fulfilled (find contentment and happiness) when we feel we are doing what is ours to do in life.
3) Life has meaning under all circumstances, even the most miserable ones. It is our responsibility to respond to life's demands to the best of our ability.

Inherent in these tenets is the conviction that human life has inestimable **value** and that it is purposeful; that each individual is **unique**, and is endowed with innate **dignity**. We are called to live with **authenticity** or integrity to fulfill our vocation of destiny, our unique meaning; and, life offers opportunities to find meaning in every situation. The task to uncover them is ours. Frankl sees happiness as a by-product to the search for meaning. **Happiness** cannot be pursued directly, rather, it ensues as the result of meaning-centered living. This tenet is also echoed by another notable voice, Helen Keller's. Out of her own experience she could say with conviction, "Many persons have a wrong idea of what constitutes true happiness. It is not attained through self-gratification but through fidelity to a worthy purpose."

Dimensions of Human Existence

In logotherapy the human being is seen as a unity comprised of body (soma), psyche (intellect and emotions), and spirit (noös).

To emphasize this unity or oneness, Frankl speaks of "dimensions of human existence." Our body, psyche, and spirit are three inseparable dimensions, unified. If one is disregarded, we do not get a complete human being but a shadowy two-dimensional projection. Disregard the spirit and you get a shadow, a caricature, an automaton of reflexes, a helpless victim of reactions and instincts, a product of drives, heredity, and environment (Fabry, 1987, p. 20).

Frankl believed, "Hitherto psychotherapy has given too little attention to the spiritual reality of man. For the aim of the psychotherapist should be to bring out the ultimate possibilities of the patient, to realize his latent values. The aphorism of the poet, Goethe, which might well be adopted as the maxim of psychotherapy, states, 'If we take people as they are, we make them worse. If we treat them as if they were what they ought to be, we help them become what they are capable of becoming'" (Frankl, 1986, DS, p.8).

To help demonstrate this concept of ontological differences and the anthropological unity, Frankl resorted to physics and geometry to depict qualitative differences, which do not destroy the unity of a structure (Frankl, 1970, WM, 22-23). Figures 3a and 3b graphically illustrate this concept. Frankl explains the diagram depicting dimensional ontology and anthropology (Fig. 3a) in this manner:

> "One and the same phenomenon projected out of its own dimension into different dimensions lower than its own is depicted in such a way that the individual pictures contradict one another." He continues, "Imagine a cylinder, say, a cup. Projected out of its three-dimensional space into the horizontal and vertical two-dimensional planes, it yields in the first case a circle and in the second one a rectangle. These pictures contradict one another. What is even more

DIMENSIONAL ONTOLOGY AND ANTHROPOLOGY
(Frankl, 1969/1988)

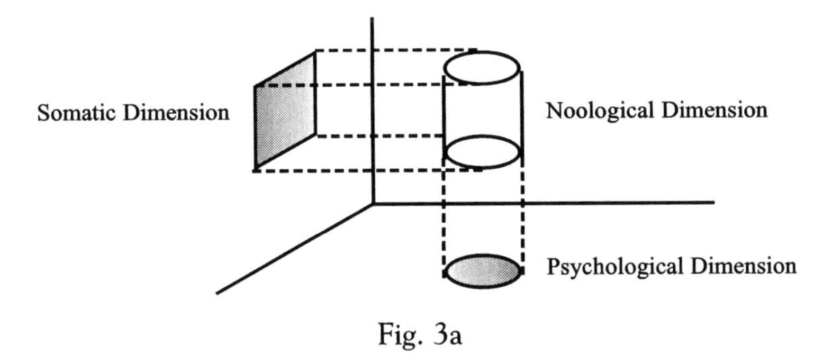

Fig. 3a

A figure projected out of its dimension into lower dimensions results in inconsistensies.

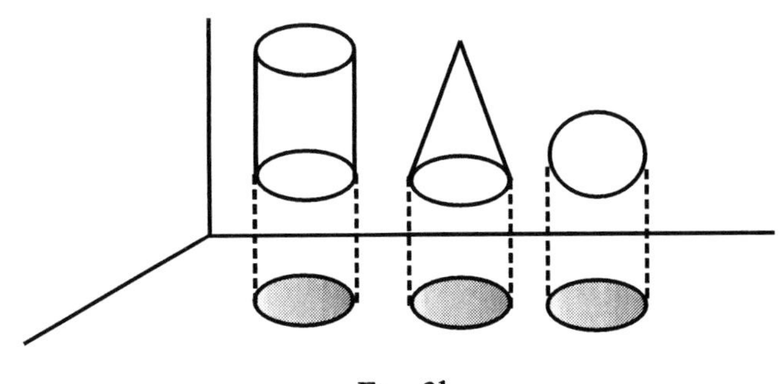

Fig. 3b

Different figures projected into a lower dimension result in isomorphies. The figures have the same form and are, therefore, ambiguous.

> important, the cup is an open vessel in contrast to the circle and the rectangle which are closed figures. Another contradiction!" (Frankl, 1970, p. 23).

In the next representation (Fig. 3b) different phenomena are projected out of their own dimension into one dimension lower than their own. As a result, they become ambiguous. Frankl explicates, "Imagine a cylinder, a cone, and a sphere. The shadows they cast upon the horizontal plane depict them as three circles which are interchangeable. We cannot infer from a shadow what casts it, what is above it, whether a cylinder, a cone, or a sphere... the projection of different phenomena into a lower dimension results in isomorphies" (1970, WM, p. 24). Frankl goes on to elaborate further:

> Dimensional ontology is far from solving the mind-body problem. But it does explain why the mind-body problem cannot be solved. Of necessity the unity of man—a unity in spite of the multiplicity of body and mind—cannot be found in the biological or psychological but must be sought in that noölogical dimension out of which man is projected in the first place (Frankl, 1988, WM, pp. 24-25).

In spite of all the ontological variations of the somatic, psychic, and noetic, the anthropological unity and wholeness of a human being is preserved and saved as soon as we turn from an analysis of existence to what Frankl calls **dimensional ontology**. His view of human beings is that we exist on many dimensions simultaneously. As in the graphically depicted analogy, it could be said that the human exists as a "diversity in unity," (Frankl, PE, p. 135). None of these dimensions must be neglected. Neither the somatic nor the psychic alone represent the genuine human; they are partial representations of the human being, projections of the higher ontological dimension, the noetic, upon the lower plane. "A higher dimension, by definition," Frankl states, "is a more *inclusive* one. The lower dimension is included in the higher one; it is subsumed in it and encompassed by it. Thus biology is overarched by psychology, psychology by noölogy..." (Frankl, 1985, UG, 13). Each of these planes or dimensions has its own characteristics:

The ***somatic dimension*** or physical plane of human beings encompasses the organic action of cells, the chemical and physical processes, the biological-physiological functions of the body; the regeneration and death of cells and the entire material organism.

The ***psychic dimension*** or plane of awareness is the sphere of emotions and the intellect. Emotional states, sensations and drives, instincts, desires, passions as well as intellectual talents, acquired behavior patterns and social impressions are housed there.

The ***noetic dimension*** is that "specifically human dimension" where such faculties as freedom of choice, intentionality (decisions of the will), creative and artistic interest, religious encounters, ethical sensitivity, conscience, understanding of values and love, the capacity to be awed by experiences, intuition and inspiration, and the search for meaning are at home.

☙

How this "diversity in unity" of different ontological dimensions is experienced is beautifully illustrated in the following parable by Dr. Elizabeth Lukas:

> Imagine sitting in a concert hall listening to a piano sonata by Beethoven. To produce this wonderful piece of music a piano is necessary, because without an instrument even the

> most exquisite composition cannot be heard. The physical presence of the piano is needed but is not enough. In this sense it can be compared to our body. What the sonata also needs is a pianist with the ability to play the composition without mistakes. But even piano-plus-pianist is not enough to perform the Beethoven sonata. The pianist can perform, but without the score the meaningful flow of sounds is missing. Arbitrarily played sounds do not produce a harmonious musical structure. The ability of the pianist to play the keys is comparable to our psychological functions which influence the body but have no higher and meaningful content. Now the dimension of the spirit comes into the picture: the composition. Only the composition unites the piano and the pianist into a meaningful totality; it makes the piano important as the carrier of the music, and it enables the pianist to transform an idea into a beautiful acoustic experience. In the same way spirit brings about a meaningful interplay between body and psyche. When the composition has been played to the end and the last sound fades in the concert hall, piano and pianist become single factors again; the union is dissolved. This parable illustrates the danger of reducing human nature to a mere physio-psychological dimension. It is as if we had said: Music is "nothing but" hitting keys, or music is "nothing but" steel strings (Lukas, 1984, p. 21).

The noetic dimension must be included to view the human being in his or her entirety. To disregard the spiritual dimension is reductionism. Joseph Fabry gives a vivid portrayal of reductionism:

> To disregard the spiritual dimension is reductionism, which Frankl considers at the root of our malaise of feeling

> empty and that life is devoid of meaning. In *Homo Patiens* he wrote as early as 1950: 'If we consider man merely as a machine ruled by conditioned reflexes, then anthropology is degraded to an annex of zoology, and the ontology of man becomes the doctrine of certain animals whose ability to walk on their hind legs has gone to their heads' (1987, p. 21)

Fabry goes on to say that the danger of such reductionism has never been greater than it is today. The biological sciences have discovered that indeed we are 'programmed' by our genetic setup and determined by our glandular functions, chemical reactions, and electrical charges. The social sciences are telling us we are the product of social and economic forces that move us about like pawns in a chess game. And psychology informs us about the drives and instincts that push us around whether we want it or not and about the various conditioning processes that determine our behavior... As an existential philosopher, Frankl explores existence from the point of view of personal experience (pp. 21-22).

Frankl does not deny that biological, social, and psychological forces exert great influence, explains Fabry, and he asserts that "man is determined, but never pandetermined." He maintains that even under the most restrictive circumstances we have an area in which we can determine our actions, our experiences or, at least, our attitudes; and this freedom of self-determination rests in the noetic realm (Fabry, 1987, p. 23). Frankl is as opposed to the psychological notion that humans are totally determined as he is to reductionism, which disregards the most vital dimension of human existence, the dimension of the spirit.

Wholeness Model of Integrated Dimensions

A further attempt at conceptualizing and graphically portraying human consciousness is made by Frankl. He depicts the noetic dimension as the innermost core in an ontological model of awareness that is spirit-centered and all inclusive (Fig. 4.). First Frankl shows the prevalent concept of *strata* of consciousness ranging from: conscious, preconscious, and unconscious. Then he depicts the model of *layers* of concentric circles of awareness, as propounded by Max Scheler: somatic, psychic, and noetic or spiritual.

By integrating the *strata* model and the *layer* model of concentric circles, Frankl devises a model of *wholeness* that is centered around a spiritual core. This spiritual/noetic axis then would extend, together with the peripheral layers encompassing it, throughout the unconscious, preconscious, and conscious stratum of awareness. Wholeness in this context means integration of the somatic, psychic, and spiritual/noetic dimensions. Only this threefold wholeness makes the human being complete. Centered around this noetic core is the person, who is not only the agent, but also the "center" of spiritual activity. In this sense the person "has" a psychophysical overlay, but the person "is" a spiritual self. The borders of these dimensions are fluid; and, there is constant transition from one to the other even though this interchange is essentially unconscious (Frankl, 1985, UG, 26-29).

Logotherapy endeavors to reach that inner noetic core through its therapeutic interventions. Its intent is to bring about healing. Viktor Frankl was quick to point out to his listeners, "The medicine chest of the logotherapist lies in the noetic dimension, the dimension of the human spirit!" He went on to emphasize that the resources of inner strengths are to be found in that dimension.

WHOLENESS MODEL OF INTEGRATED DIMENSIONS
(Based on Frankl, 1975/1985, UG, p. 29)

Strata of awareness:

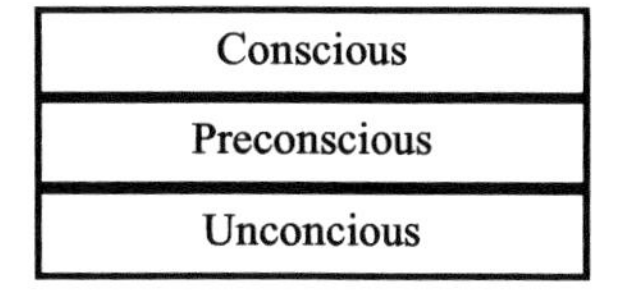

Layers of concentric circles:

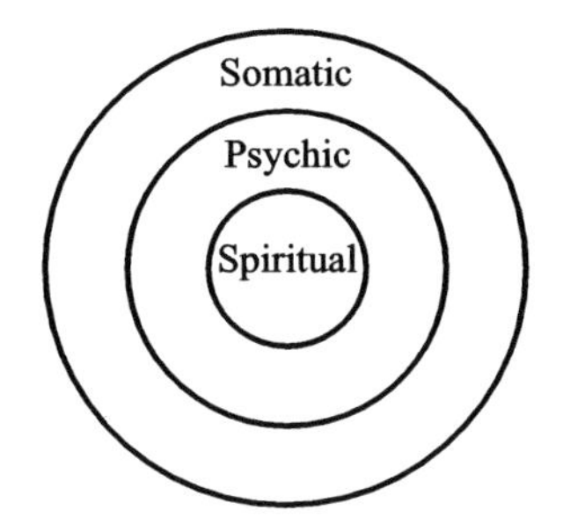

Integrating the *strata* model and *layers* model=
Frankl's *wholeness* model

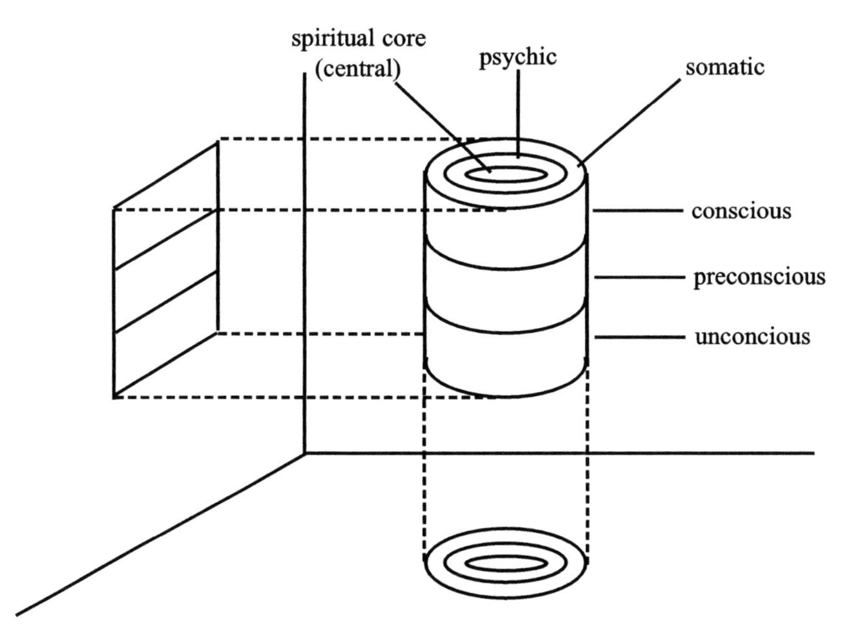

Fig. 4

These strengths must be activated in order to bring about transformation in a person.

In a professional field that is an intuitive art, as well as a learned craft, the therapist walks a fine line. If the craft is overdeveloped at the exclusion of the art, there is danger of it becoming rote; i.e., going with standard formulations and techniques. If the art of the therapeutic process is overemphasized, the process may become vague and without direction. Therefore, heart and head must walk hand-in-hand in logotherapy. At times the head may have to lead, at other times the heart. If the head predominates, not only compassion, but also insight and intuition, and perception of the uniqueness of each person may be lost. When the heart leads, there is danger of emotionalism that does not lead anywhere therapeutically beyond catharsis. The mental and emotional regions of the psychic dimension must be connected to and integrated with the noetic or spiritual core where the "medicine chest" of the logotherapist can be found.

Help from the Noetic Dimension

In *The Pursuit of Meaning* (1987), which could have been subtitled, "Logotherapy Explained," Joseph Fabry further clarified the concept of the noetic dimension and the therapeutic help available therein:

> The concept of the noetic dimension helps us understand and improve ourselves and helps the therapist understand and improve mental health. The therapist must try to reach this human dimension in patients because it contains the core of their humanity. According to logotherapy, sickness can originate in our *noos*; but unlike our body and psyche, the *noos*, our spirit, can never become sick. This is what

> Frankl calls his first, his psychiatric, credo: the belief that the noetic person exists even behind the curtain of the symptoms of a psychotic illness (p. 25).

Fabry goes on to say that the logotherapist elicits help from the patient's noetic center, even if it is buried by a mountain of psychophysical symptoms. The defiant power of the human spirit is evoked to rebel against seemingly all-powerful forces of the psyche and the body. This is Frankl's second, his psychotherapeutic, credo: the belief that not only the noetic part of the person remains well even if the surrounding psychophysical area has become sick but also that the noetic self has the power to rise above the afflictions of the psychophysical self. Patients may not be able to change their condition, but they *can* change their attitude toward their own, perhaps incurably sick, psychophysical area (25-26).

Three particular areas related to the noetic dimension are pointed to as having therapeutic significance: the noetic unconscious; the intuitive conscience; and, self-transcendence. These topics were addressed in *Meaning-Centered Interventions* (Rice, Graber, Pitts, Rogina & Sjolie. 2002) and are presented here with modifications:

The Noetic Unconscious

Frankl sees the noetic part of the unconscious as a region in which we are not an ego driven by an id but a self, a person relating to others as human beings to be loved and understood rather than things to be used and manipulated. It is in the noetic realm of our unconscious that we experience what it truly means to be human. The noetic unconscious is the source for our artistic inspiration, our religious faith, our beliefs, and our intuitions. It is in this realm that we gain our sense of direction and meaning in life. It is the home of "authentic self" rather than id or superego.

The noetic dimension contains the essence of life and the noetic unconscious contains the voice of meaning. As pointed out, the noetic dimension is like the medicine chest of logotherapy containing the resources of the human spirit:

- Our will to meaning with its inherent freedom of choice
- Our goals and purposes in life
- Our creativity
- Our capacity to love (beyond the physical)
- Our consciousness
- Our sense of humor
- Our commitment to tasks
- Our ideas and ideals
- Our imagination
- Our responsibility and response-ability
- Our self-awareness
- Our compassion
- Our ability to forgive
- Our awareness of mortality

The noetic unconscious might be understood as the reservoir of these resources. This is the place within our humanness where we hear the call to meaning in the circumstances and events of our lives. As Frankl states in *Man's Search for Ultimate Meaning* (1997), "Authentic existence is present where a self is deciding for itself, but not where an id is driving it." (32). When self is deciding for itself, the noetic unconscious is having its say.

The Intuitive Conscience

In *The Will to Meaning* (1988), Frankl states that meaning cannot be given arbitrarily but must be found responsibly. He also tells us that meaning must be sought for conscientiously. Humans are guided in the search for meaning by conscience. Conscience could be defined as the intuitive capacity of man to find out the meaning of a situation (p. 18-19). Since a generalized meaning cannot possibly be given to the myriad of situations and experiences in each unique life, an intuitive capacity such as conscience is the only means for grasping the meaning of any moment. Frankl's concept of intuitive conscience is that it is the key element of self-transcendence, which helps the self to discover unique meanings and ethical values in a variety of existential situations that demand choices (Gould, 1993, p. 10).

The human experience calls for an ability to make independent and authentic decisions at each moment in life. To live responsibly calls for listening to the thousands of commandments arising from the thousands of unique situations of which life consists. It is the intuitive conscience that guides us in the moment by moment experiences of life. It gives voice to the available resources of the sprit within.

Self-Transcendence

Viktor Frankl sees self-transcendence as one of the two unique capacities of human beings, self-detachment being the other [self-detachment will be addressed at length in Chapter VI]. Self-transcendence refers to the ability to rise above and beyond self regarding outward conditions. In *The Doctor and the Soul* (1986), Frankl states that human existence points to and is directed toward something or someone other than oneself, "...namely, meanings to fulfill, or toward other human beings to encounter lovingly. Only to the extent to which a human being lives out his self-transcendence is he really becoming human and actualizing himself" (p. 294). An additional clarifying statement comes from *The Unconscious God* (1975) where Frankl writes, "What I have called the self-transcendence of existence denotes the fundamental fact that being human means relating to something, or someone, other than oneself, be it a meaning to fulfill, or human beings to encounter. And existence falters and collapses unless this self-transcendent quality is lived out" (p. 47).

It is within the context of self-transcendence that individuals experience the areas of life where meaning is available. For example, self-discovery, choice, uniqueness, and responsibility are often experienced through self-transcendence. Additionally, as pointed out by Fabry, transcending self provides meaning in exactly the area where an individual feels defeated. That is to say, defeat can be turned into victory. However, there is an inherent problem. It is difficult to transcend self when life has been difficult. "How can you be motivated to transcend your instinctive egocentricity? Why should you do anything for others, when life has dealt unkindly with you?" (Fabry, 1988, *Guideposts to Meaning*, p. 85) Addressing this concern is part of the work of logotherapy (Rice et al., 2002, Chap. VI).

Recapitulation: What is Logotherapy?

Having reached the end of this chapter, in case the reader would like a simple explanation of logotherapy, the most concise answer to this question the author has found comes from Viktor Frankl himself. In *Man's Search for Meaning* he gave the following answer when asked to explain logotherapy:

> Let me explain why I have employed the term 'logotherapy' as the name for my theory. *Logos* is a Greek word which denotes 'meaning.' [The student of religion is more familiar with Logos being translated as the "Word" or "Will" of God].

> Logotherapy or, as it has been called by some authors, 'The Third Viennese School of Psychotherapy,' focuses on the meaning of human existence as well as on man's search for such a meaning. According to logotherapy, this striving to find a meaning in one's life is the primary motivational force in man (1985, p. 121).

The search for meaning will have to be based on authenticity as a prerequisite. That which is meaningful will have real value for a person; it will be congruent with who s/he is; it will be pursued with commitment. In order for the pursuit of meaning to be of value, it will need to be accomplished with integrity. Logotherapy offers a challenge to leave peripheral falsehoods behind on the journey to that which is at the spiritual center, at the nucleus of the personality—the *Logos*.

V

MEANING-CENTERED ORIENTATION of LOGOTHERAPY

Toward a Consciousness of Responsibility

Frankl held that logotherapy is ultimately education toward responsibility; that the person must push toward the concrete meaning of his own existence. He likened this journey in awareness to the progression from psychotherapy to logotherapy and the aim of his existential analysis in this manner:

> Psychotherapy endeavors to bring instinctual facts to consciousness. Logotherapy, on the other hand, seeks to bring to awareness the spiritual realities. As existential analysis it is particularly concerned with making men conscious of their responsibility—since being responsible is one of the essential grounds of human existence. If to be human is, as we have said, to be conscious and responsible, then existential analysis is psychotherapy whose starting-point is consciousness of responsibility (Frankl, 1975, DS, p. 25).

As we expand our consciousness toward embracing our responsibilities, a further distinction is made between responsibility that is externally demanded of us and our ability to go even beyond that which is required of us. This ability to respond not only to outer mandates, but to inner convictions, is the hallmark of the more fully developed consciousness. Here response-ability to seek out what is most meaningful, along with the commitment to carrying it out, becomes a way of life.

Responding to External and Internal Authority

Regarding response-ability, a further distinction is made in logotherapy between *responsibility* and *responsibleness*. Responsibility is seen as imposed from the outside—"I should." Responsibleness is a freely chosen response to an inner knowing—"I ought." From the past we have inherited cultural values that mandated responsibility. These values or cultural norms came from church, family and society, and exerted considerable authoritative influence. They were accepted and not questioned. Today we enjoy a greater measure of personal freedom from external authority, but we need to develop authority from within. Responsibleness refers to that inner dictum. We respond not because we are forced to, but because we decide to respond. "Freedom from" rejects outside authority while "freedom to" requires self-imposed authority from within.

When we defy values offered by family, church, or society without finding a center of meaning within, we are adrift. Unprepared to direct our own lives we often feel abandoned, bored, empty, and depressed. Frankl relates to us that unlike other animals we are not told by drives and instincts what to do. If we have not developed an internal locus of authority, we may not know what we want to do. As a result we either do what other people do, *conformism*; or we do what other people want us to do, *totalitarianism*. In either case our freedom is lost (Fabry, 1987, 120-127).

Meanings and Values

Areas where *meanings* and *values* can be discovered in life that will lead to a consciousness of responsibility were outlined by

Frankl. He differentiates between "meanings" and "values" from which we continuously respond. The distinction between meanings and values was developed gradually by Frankl. In his earlier writings these terms are used almost synonymously. Later he began to differentiate, assigning a broader spectrum to values, and a more specific definition to meanings. Values have "universal meanings," they are held in common by a large group of people in a given time. For example, in our contemporary urban culture, stopping at a red light is a commonly accepted value that is held to be meaningful by most. As such, it has become the standard response, a value held in common, by people in cultures with vehicular traffic and congestion at intersections. Stopping at a red light would not have held any meaning for anyone living before we had motorized vehicles or intersections that required traffic lights. Values change to accommodate the needs of people when they no longer offer "universal meanings."

When it comes to "unique meanings" based on individual discernment (having specific value for a person), those meanings are not readily transmittable to other persons or situations. In his autobiography, *Viktor Frankl: Recollections*, Dr. Frankl relates his agonizing process, in 1941, of discerning whether or not to leave Vienna where he knew he was in danger of incarceration by the Nazi regime. He describes how (after waiting years for a visa to emigrate to the United States) he came to a decision in this manner:

> ...Finally, shortly before Pearl Harbor, I was asked to come to the American Consulate to pick up my visa. Then I hesitated. Should I leave my parents behind? I knew what their fate would be: deportations to a concentration camp. Should I say goodbye, and leave them to their fate? The visa applied to me alone.
>
> Undecided, I left home, took a walk, and had this thought: 'Isn't this the kind of situation that requires some

> hint from heaven?' When I returned home, my eyes fell on a little piece of marble lying on the table.
>
> 'What's this?' I asked my father.
>
> 'This? Oh, I picked it out of the rubble of the synagogue they have burned down. It has on it part of the Ten Commandments. I can tell you from which commandment it comes. There is only one commandment that uses the letter that is chiseled here.'
>
> 'And that is..?' I asked eagerly.
>
> Then father gave me this answer: 'Honor thy father and thy mother, that thy days may be long upon the land which the Lord thy God giveth thee' (Frankl, 1997, 82).

Frankl concludes by saying that he stayed 'upon the land' with his parents, and let the visa lapse. He muses, "It may be that I made my decision deep within, long before, and that the oracle was in reality only an echo from the voice of my conscience" (p. 83).

Here is an example of a choice that held "unique meanings." It was a deeply meaningful choice for Viktor Frankl personally. It was a courageous choice, a heroic choice, made in the face of tremendous risk. It certainly had dire consequences for him. It led to his deportation to the concentration camp. Yet, he maintains, it was the right choice for him to make—it brought him inner peace.

While choices having "unique meanings" for a person are in harmony with the general value structure of the society, there is no conflict. Conflict arises when individual meanings and the values held in common by others collide. Following standard values and conforming to general norms, rather than finding the unique meaning of a situation, simplifies life; but, it may prove costly when it results in inner conflict.

Ultimate Meaning, Meaning of the Moment

Logotherapy sees meaning being experienced on two levels: ultimate meaning and the meaning of the moment. The first, *ultimate meaning*, is experienced as a universal order in which every person has a place. This order is seen in either religious or secular terms, depending on one's world view. To this first order, the ultimate questions of life are addressed: "Who am I?"; "What is my purpose?"; "Where am I going?"; "How will I get there?"; and, "How do I fit into the whole scheme of life?" The existence of ultimate meaning cannot be proved, except in the unrepeatable experimentation of living. The proof does not come from ever reaching and holding the meaning of life—which is as impossible as reaching and holding the ever-receding horizon—the proof lies in the fulfillment that comes with the search (Fabry, 1987, p.xv). Fabry continues, "This grandiose order, I believe, is what Frankl understands by *logos*, ultimate meaning. We can never hope to 'find' it in its totality, we can only pursue it to the best of our abilities" (Fabry, 1987, p. 5). When Frankl refers to *ultimate meaning*, he makes clear that at this point we pass from the psyche to the spiritual dimension. "The ultimate meaning of man's life is not a matter of his intellectual cognition, but rather of his existential commitment... Man takes a stand and makes a choice" (Frankl, 1985, PE, 84).

The other order of meaning is much easier to comprehend, the *meaning of the moment*. This is a meaning that is readily found in daily situations. Logotherapy offers a daring concept: Each person is a unique individual, going from birth to death through a string of unique life situations. Every situation, every unrepeatable moment, offers a specific meaning potential. To respond to these meaning offerings of the moment is to lead a meaningful life. In most situations the *meaning of the moment* is nothing spectacular; it's the daily routine. Some moments are subtler than others. Some offer bigger choices than others. The meaning of the moment differs from moment to moment, and from person to person. By and large, they are the small daily events of life (Fabry, 1987, xvi, 37). When speaking of the *meaning of the moment*, Frankl has referred to the hour glass. The sands of time do not move upward, nor do they stop until death. Therefore, each moment presents a new, unique situation to which we must respond. We can seize the moment or miss it (Welter, 1995, IX).

Demand Quality of Life

Both *ultimate meaning* and the *meanings of the moment* place demands upon us. Logotherapy sees us as always reaching out, pursuing goals. Human existence, always points at something beyond itself... a meaning to fulfill, another human being to encounter. Frankl calls this the demand quality of life. In this connection Frankl quotes a famous passage by Hillel, "If I don't do it, who will do it? If I don't do it now, when shall I do it? And if I do it for myself [alone], what am I?" (Fabry, 1987, 38-39).

The *demand quality of life*, in view of the hourglass analogy, clearly points to the present moment. The sands of time march through the narrow part single-file, moment by moment. The future becomes the past only after it has passed through the present, the "here and now." The present is the only time there is in which existential commitments can be carried out. Only then can the meanings gleaned from these actions be deposited into the past.

Frankl poetically reiterates, "In the past nothing is irrevocably lost but everything is irrevocably stored. People only see the stubble field of transitoriness but overlook the full granaries of the past in which they have delivered and deposited, in which they have saved the harvest" (1970, WM, p. 156).

THE DEMAND QUALITY OF LIFE

What is life asking of me?

The future holds the challenges with their meaning possibilities. How I respond to these demands life will place on me will determine what kind of person I become.

FUTURE

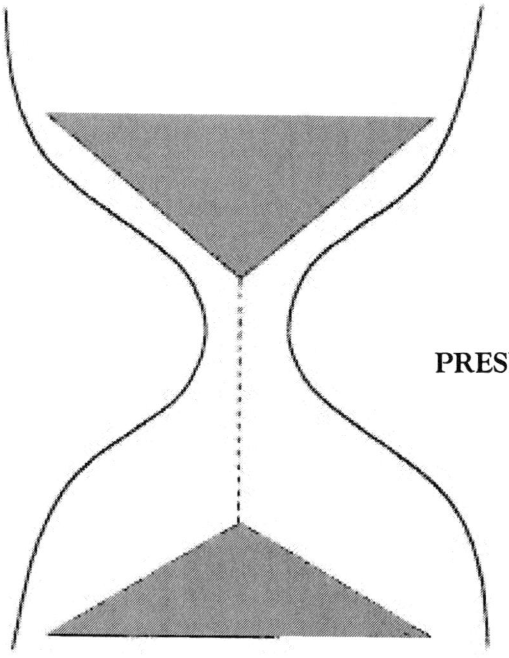

PRESENT

Moment by moment
I qualify my life
as time and
its events flow by,
on their way
from the future
to the past.
Only in the
"here and now"
can I take a stand
or take action and
respond to the demands
life places before me.

PAST

Fig. 5

The sands of time do not move upward, but flow through the narrow passage of the present single-file. Moment by moment, the future becomes the past, as it passes through the "here and now" of the present to be stored in the past forever.

To emphasize the unique role conscience plays in living responsibly by meeting the demand quality of life, Frankl gives the following description:

> Meaning cannot be given arbitrarily but must be found responsibly. I could have said as well that it must be sought for conscientiously. And in fact man is guided in his search for meaning by conscience. Conscience could be defined as the intuitive capacity of man to find out the meaning of a situation. Since this meaning is something unique, it does not fall under a general law, and an intuitive capacity such as conscience is the only means to seize hold of meaning Gestalts. Apart from being intuitive, conscience is creative. Time and again, an individual's conscience commands him to do something which contradicts what is preached by the society to which the individual belongs (1970, WM, p. 63).

To illustrate his point regarding meanings and values, Frankl tells this story of someone who belongs to a tribe of cannibals; an individual's creative conscience may well find out that, in a given situation, it is more meaningful to spare the life of an enemy than to kill him. This way his conscience may well start a revolution, in that what is at first a unique meaning may become a universal value–'Thou shalt not kill.' The unique meaning of today is the universal value of tomorrow. This is the way ... values evolve (1970, WM, p. 63).

Gathering from Frankl's description, values are not static but ever changing, and thereby transforming human consciousness. Their driving force is the meaning they harbor. When values become devoid of meaning, they are discarded and gradually replaced with dynamic and pertinent ones that are meaningful to the person or the group that conceived them.

Ways of Discovering Meaning: The Meaning Triangle

The meanings which we human beings strive to attain can be found in our responses to life. Once we realize that we are unique, have readily available resources in the form of talents, capabilities and inner strengths, we are no longer totally at the mercy of fate. Realizing that we have areas of freedom (however small they may be) and that we have choices in response to the demands life places upon us, we cannot remain in the victim stance any longer. Yet, meanings cannot be arbitrarily invented, they must be discovered. Frankl points to three ways of discovering meaning:

1) by creating a work or accomplishing a task;
2) by experiencing something in life (such as goodness, truth, and beauty) or by encountering another person in the uniqueness of the other's existence through love; or
3) by the attitude that a person takes toward unavoidable suffering (Frankl, 1959, MSM, p. 133-134).

Creativity

The first way is perhaps the best known. It is the way to meaning we travel when we engage in life through our talents. With it comes the fulfillment we experience from a goal reached, a task mastered, a job well done. This way to meaning is as readily available to us as we are willing to respond to the tasks life places before us. Through applying our creativity, our unique talents and strengths, we can be vitally engaged in life and find life well worth living–in other words, meaningful. This avenue to meaning is like an open invitation extended to us to give our return to Life through the gifts with which we were endowed. Utilizing this avenue can lead to deep fulfillment as well as to the discovery of our innate endowments, and to the development of their potential to the fullest.

Experiences

The second way to discovering meaning is found through experiences: encountering others in relationships of various kinds; also through experiences with nature, culture or religion. Logotherapy states that experiencing can be as valuable as achieving or realizing value through creativity. Here we receive from Life without any effort on our part. This avenue compensates for the one-sided emphasis on the external world of achievement at the expense of the internal world of experience. Frankl reminds us that meaning can be found not only in work but also in love (Frankl, 1985, MSM, p. 170). Loving entails coming into relationship with another as a spiritual being. This includes the love for God and religious experiences.

Attitude

Frankl calls the third way, finding meaning in unavoidable suffering, the noblest appreciation of meaning and the deepest possible meaning. When a person chooses to rise above the circumstances of life and to use the experience as an opportunity to grow, the attitude that a person takes toward suffering turns the situation into an achievement, a triumph of heroism. The reason that life is never devoid of meaning is because even when creative or experiential ways of finding meaning are not possible, a person is still challenged to find meaning in the midst of suffering by suffering with dignity (Frankl, 1969, WTM, p. 70). Logotherapy's emphasis on attitudinal values gives an incurable sufferer the opportunity to ennoble his or her suffering by bearing it courageously rather than feeling degraded because of it. Thus, meaning ensues from the attitude brought toward the blows of fate.

Reflections on the Meaning Triangle

The three ways to discovering meaning, namely creativity, experience, and attitude, are sometimes referred to as *The Meaning Triangle*. The author devised a self-appraisal tool based on the "meaning triangle." When a simple method was needed to assess client recources, *Reflections on the Meaning Triangle* was developed. It is used to help clients recall that they do have resources which have served them well in the past. These same qualities can be brought to bear on current life situations that may be difficult. Getting in touch with these qualities dissipates the feeling of helplessness and hopelessness. It moves the client into an awareness of strengths, capabilities, talents and a host of overlooked resources. It fosters a "*Yes, I can!*" attitude, instead of the deadly, "*I can't*."

Reflections on the Meaning Triangle is a non-invasive, non-threatening way to get to know client strengths. Even the most despairing will find resources in at least one area of their "meaning triangle" or recall a time in their lives when they did experience life as meaningful. This strengths awareness tool can be used individually or in a group format as an introductory instrument that focuses on "what's right" about me and avoids an endless recitation of "what's wrong" with me. It has been successfully used at the beginning of therapy with individuals and with diverse groups.

A sampling of responses given to Reflections on the Meaning Triangle will bear out the usefulness of this tool when a quick and simple method is needed. It has been used as a conversational method informally, and as a written instrument when time and space allowed. Respondents' answers to the three questions are as varied and unique as the responders themselves. Here are some of the responses received.

REFLECTIONS ON THE MEANING TRIANGLE

(Based on Viktor Frankl's Logotherapy)

A Strengths Awareness Instrument

Three ways of finding meaning in life are represented as angles of a triangle—***The Meaning Triangle***. Each angle encompasses one way to meaning:

1. What I give to life through my **creativity**.
2. What I receive from life through **experiences**.
3. The stance I take toward life through my **attitude**.

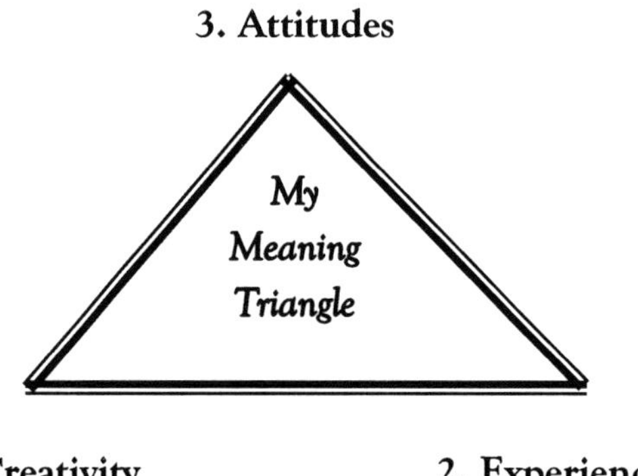

Reflecting upon the following questions will help you to discover meaning experienced at some time in your life. Answer the following questions with the first impression that comes to mind.

1. ***What creative gifts have I offered to others through my talents, my work, deeds done, goals achieved that held meaning for me?***

2. ***What experiences have I received from encountering others in relationships of all kinds, from nature, culture or religion that were deeply meaningful?***

3. ***What attitudinal values have I realized by taking a stance toward situations or blows of fate that was courageous or self-transcending?***

Fig. 6

1. The first question—dealing with the area of **creativity**—asks:

What creative gifts have I offered to others through my talents, my work, deeds done, goals achieved that held meaning for me?

One woman wrote:

"When life was closing doors an every front, I found I still had one skill left—something I learned from my grandmother and was proud of: I could still make soup! It was a meaningful use of my time and talent because it not only fed us, but it may have saved my sanity. At least, while I was immersed in soup-making, I felt worthwhile as a person."

A middle aged man recalls a cherished goal achieved early in life and the triumphant feeling derived from it that still serves him well:

"I must have been twelve at the time. I hit my first home run. What joy! I felt so alive! So triumphant! It was a great moment. Suddenly I knew how it felt to achieve a cherished goal after much hard work and practice. It became a reference point for me not to give up when at first I didn't succeed, but to persevere in difficult struggles."

A therapeutic encounter with a disheartened client can be summed up as follows:

A discouraged mother, worn out and overburdened with rearing children, felt she was a total failure. When she was asked to name a worthwhile goal she had achieved at some point in her life, she couldn't think of anything. It was pointed out to her that she was obviously well educated; she then straightened in her seat and began to tell of her long and difficult road to earn a master's degree; how slow and arduous and—in retrospect—very meaningful it had been. With that realization, she began to see herself in a different light... she had succeeded in fulfilling her cherished dream to educate herself. Hope was kindled that she just might be in the long arduous phase of child rearing right now, and that eventually she would be able to look back with pride and joy, and see this as a time when she responsibly fulfilled a major life task–one day at a time. This realization restored her courage to go on.

The above examples all fit into the category of creativity - giving of oneself. To be creative implies having the courage to act on a creative impulse and bring it responsibly to its fruition. The pursuit of something that is personally meaningful will result in fulfillment, in finding meaning.

☙

2. The second question–addressing **experiences**–seeks to know:

What experiences have I received from encountering others in relationships of all kinds, from nature, culture or religion that were deeply meaningful?

A mother described a tremendously uplifting cultural experience in this moving paragraph:

"After weeks of caring for our gravely ill child, my husband urged me one evening to go to the symphony while he took over at our son's bedside. Although I felt guilty leaving them alone, it turned out to be the best thing I could have done. I had always resonated to the music of Beethoven. That evening I experienced his Ninth Symphony as never before. The chorus carried me to the Elysian Fields of which they sang. I experienced something sublime. I felt renewed–ready to return to take my place at the bedside of our ill child."

Love of nature and animals is often cited as providing experiences that come to us without our having to do anything. A sunrise or sunset, scenery that inspires awe needs only to be enjoyed. It does not demand anything of us–it is a gift.

Regarding the love of animals, a young boy answered the above question in this manner:

"I can't wait to get off the school bus in the afternoon because my dog is waiting for me to play. When we play, I forget all my troubles." This troubled youngster can look forward to something at the end of his school day. For a little while there are no demands on him; he can just be engaged in play with his dog. Afterward he is better able to deal with what is his to do... the never-ending homework, chores, and circumstances that are beyond his control.

For some older people, when many former activities that provided meanings are no longer possible, religious experiences become valued sources of meaning. The following example will demonstrate how the practice of religion became a vital source of meaning when other avenues were no longer available:

When asked about meaningful experiences in this stage of life, a housebound older lady related how she arranges her week around the communion visits by someone from her church. Not that she had been a weekly communicant all her life, but now this has become very important to her. She has time to pray and to prepare for the pastoral visit, which was not always the case in her busy life. The experience of practicing her religion has become meaningful and life-giving. Without this weekly highlight her life would be much lonelier.

An example of a meaningful moment from the treasure chest of past memories is shared with us. The recall of love shared gave courage to struggle on:

Viktor Frankl recalled how in the worst days of his life he once heard a melody, played by a lonely violin. The piece reminded him of his wife. It was her birthday. He did not know where she was, nor whether she was still alive. But that little melody brought all the rich shared experiences with the human being he loved so dearly to mind. It lifted him beyond the misery of his struggle to survive one more day in the concentration camp. The moment had great experiential value for him. It was a treasured gift life gave him that day.

The above examples demonstrate the importance of experiences and encounters with others. They are taproots through which to draw strength. Unlike creative values, experiential values make hardly any demands upon us. They come to us as gifts, asking only to be received in order to be meaningful.

☙

3. The third question explores the value **attitudes** can have by asking:

What attitudinal values have I realized by taking a stance toward situations or circumstances that was courageous or self-transcending?

Consider this heroic example of finding meaning in the attitude taken toward unavoidable suffering:

A patient was dying of an incurable disease. Knowing that she could not avoid the inescapable suffering, she determined that she could, however, determine the manner and mode in which she would meet the illness. She became a tower of strength to those around her, whose hearts were lacerated with pain. At first it was a 'bravado,' but with the passage of time the act became invested with purpose. In time she could say, 'Perhaps my single act of immortality might be in the way I face this adversity. Even though my pain at times is unbearable–I have achieved an inner peace and contentment that I had never known before.' She died in dignity and is remembered for her indomitable courage. (As told by Dr. Frankl)

A middle-aged man recalled a courageous and self-transcending action that impacted his attitude in this manner:

"A very meaningful time for me was when I marched in the grape boycotts with Chavez. Having seen the wretched conditions in which the fruit pickers lived and worked, marching on their behalf was among the best things I have done. It gave me a purpose; my idealism had an outlet. It was great. I'm glad I did it."

A young New Yorker recalls September 11, 2001, as one of the worst days of her life and one of the best because it changed her attitude about life and, consequently, her relationship to others:

J. saw the first tower burning, then watched–aghast–as the second tower was hit. Shortly thereafter she received word that her father was among the unaccounted for at the Pentagon–presumed dead. And she was forced to evacuate her dust clogged apartment immediately.

Previously J. had resented her father's military career with its disrupting effects on her life. She had also perceived New York as a cold and uncaring place; she lived there because she had found employment. All this was about to change for J. as she entered one of the hastily set up aid centers. Whatever she needed was provided for her. Top on her list: People who cared and listened....

Recovering from the shock and bewilderment of events so traumatically thrust upon her, J.'s attitude underwent a profound change. She could begin to appreciate her father for who he was as a person, not judge him only by his absences and disruptions of her early life. Having seen New Yorkers' at their best, J. will now tell you that she loves New York–and her Dad. (As told to Curt Westermann)

When we cannot escape life's problems, we have to face them. There is still one meaningful choice open to us: The **attitude** we choose in how we meet our inescapable sufferings. The meaning that is gained from taking a heroic stance toward "blows of fate" is perhaps the highest in the hierarchy of values.

The foregoing examples validate the meaning triangle's importance. In logotherapy treatment is built upon client strengths rather than pathology. *Reflections on the Meaning Triangle* is offered here as a tool to help discover them. Once an awareness of strengths has been gained, these same resources can be applied to current problems. By getting in touch with sources that held meaning once, a person is open to a transcendent dimension from where healing can come. As mentioned earlier, logotherapy looks to the core, the spiritual center, as the medicine chest. Helping to facilitate an awareness that can reach beyond current difficulties to areas where meaning can be experienced is the first step to overcoming those difficulties.

☙

Furthermore, there is a long-range meaning that encompasses an individual's entire life. Frankl uses the analogy of a movie to illustrate this point:

> "... consider a movie: it consists of thousands upon thousands of individual pictures, and each of them makes sense and carries a meaning, yet the meaning of the whole film cannot be seen before its last sequence is shown. However, we cannot understand the whole film without having first understood each of its components, each of the individual pictures. Isn't it the same with life? Doesn't the final meaning of life, too, reveal itself, if at all, only at its end, on the

> verge of death? And doesn't this final meaning too, depend on whether or not the potential meaning of each single situation has been actualized to the best of the respective individual's knowledge and belief?" (Frankl, 1959, MSM, p. 168).

Frankl believed that if meaning in life exists, then it must be an unconditional meaning that neither suffering nor dying can diminish. In psychotherapy, it is this unconditional meaning in life that leads to psychological health. What is important is the specific meaning at any particular moment in that person's life. Meaning is contained within the concrete experiences of daily life. In addition, each person has a special purpose to fulfill in life that demands to be accomplished. Each person is unique and cannot be replaced by another. There will not be a second chance to fulfill the special assignment for which the individual is responsible. The task is specific and unique as is the opportunity to accomplish the task. Each situation in life presents a challenge to face and a problem for the individual to solve. The meaning of life is always changing, but it never ceases to exist. The realization of meaning involves becoming aware of the possibilities that exist in each situation (Frankl, 1959, MSM, p.169).

Frankl states that ultimately, man should not ask what the meaning of his life is, but rather he must recognize that it is *he* who is asked. In a word, each man is questioned by life; and he can only answer to life by *answering for* his own life; to life he can only respond by being responsible. Thus, logotherapy sees in responsibleness the very essence of human existence (Frankl, 1985, MSM, p. 131).

VI

PRIMARY METHODS of LOGOTHERAPY

Fundamental Assumption: The Therapeutic Relationship

Before we even begin a discussion about the techniques or methods of logotherapy, it is well to bring to mind that no meaningful work between a counselor and client takes place before a trust bridge is established. Logotherapy builds this relationship of trust on the humanity of the client, on the human spirit with its will to meaning. From that starting point, interventions take off on a hopeful note and in faith that a meaningful future can be built from the rubble of the past. Frankl deems the therapeutic relationship, sometimes even referred to as the therapeutic friendship, as the primary ingredient in successful therapeutic interventions when he states:

> It is not so much the method, but rather the relationship between the patient and his doctor or, to use a currently popular expression, the "encounter" between the therapist and his patient. This relationship between two persons seems to be the most significant aspect of the psychotherapeutic process, a more important factor than any method or technique. However, we should not be disdainful of technique, for in therapy a certain degree of detachment on the part of the therapist is indispensable. In fact, on occasion the human element must be disregarded in order to expedite the treatment (1985, PE, p.141).

He concludes by stating that the therapeutic relationship develops in a polar field of tension in which the poles are represented by the extremes of human closeness on the one hand and scientific detachment on the other. Therefore, the therapist must beware lest he be beguiled into falling prey to the extreme of considering only one of these. This means that the therapist must neither be guided by mere sympathy, by his desire to help his patient, nor conversely repress his human interest in the other human being by dealing with him merely in terms of technique (1985, pp. 141-142).

☙

Before attempting to use the methods or techniques of logotherapy, its underlying philosophy must be understood and appreciated. As stated repeatedly, the axiom of logotherapy is that the exclusively human characteristic is the spirit, also referred to as the noetic dimension. Any attempt to utilize these methods without including the human spirit in the process, will meet with disappointment. Beginning with this self-evident truth, the practical application of logotherapy is built on premises succinctly described by Elisabeth Lukas, a foremost Franklian scholar and clinician, and is reiterated here with her kind permission:

Summary of Logotherapeutic Premises

Premise 1: The human being is three-dimensional (assuming that the first two, body and psyche, are granted).

Premise 2: In each of the three dimensions dependency on given circumstances is different: Within the biological dimension (shared with animals and plants) dependency on given circumstances is almost total and hardly manipulable. Within the psychological dimension (shared with animals) dependency on given circumstances is flexible and highly manipulable. Within the dimension of the spirit (exclusively human) there exists the possibility of a free choice of attitude toward given circumstances.

Premise 3: The three dimensions form an inseparable unit.

Premise 4: No dimension can be disregarded in psychotherapy. Psychotherapists must treat their patients in their totality, including all dimensions. Surgeons must not confine themselves to the amputation of a leg when a patient suffers from bone cancer. Nor must psychologists restrict themselves to an interpretation of test results when their clients question the meaning of life. Ministers must not limit themselves to religious wisdom when members of their congregation come to them with family problems. All members of the helping professions have an obligation to respond to genuine calls for help, if not on a professional then on a human level. If they feel incompetent in a certain area, they should refer patients to others who can provide help.

Premise 5: The feedback mechanism works differently in each of the three dimensions. Within the biological dimension, feedback mechanisms bring about automatic processes in the autonomic nervous system that help the body adapt to a changed situation. Within the psychological dimension, feedback mechanisms bring about reinforcement processes and lead to changes in behavior. Within the dimension of the spirit, feedback mechanisms bring about changes in self-understanding and lead to a new interpretation of the self.

Premise 6: For each of the three dimensions the principle of homeostasis has a different validity. Within the biological dimension the homeostasis principle is always valid. Within the psychological dimension, it is valid most of the time. Within the dimension of the spirit, it is not valid.

Nearly all theories about human nature see homeostasis, the absence of tension, as a desirable therapeutic goal. Frankl, however, points out that in the dimension of the spirit homeostasis is not a desirable condition but rather a warning signal of existential frustration. A tensionless state in the spirit would denote complete satisfaction, a lack of goals. Goals beckon only when conditions are not completely satisfying and leave room for change. When people lack the necessity to change, to create, to finish a project, to experience, or at least to brave unchanging fate, the need to live may be questioned.

Frankl speaks of a "healthy noodynamism," a field of tension between what we are and our vision of becoming. Such noetic tension stands in opposition to being in balance with ourselves and the world. Balance is enormously important for all life forms, but for human beings it is not enough (Lukas, 1984, 27-28).

Of the above outlined fundamental premises the sixth premise, addressing the concept of "healthy noodynamism" or "noodynamic tension," is particularly noteworthy because it is here that logotherapy departs from most other counseling theories. Having gained a thorough understanding of the foregoing we can turn our attention to the methods applied in logotherapy.

Techniques Employed in Logotherapy

There are four primary methods or distinct approaches used in logotherapeutic interventions. In addition, innovative applications of many other existing psychotherapeutic methods, which are compatible with logotherapy's understanding of the human being, are employed. Some of them will be discussed later. The four primary techniques utilized are:

- Self-Distancing
- Paradoxical Intention
- Socratic Dialogue
- Dereflection

Depending on the nature of the presenting problem one of these methods will be most appropriate. Usually they are used in combination in the therapeutic protocol.

Self-Distancing

When clients present with their problems or symptoms, the first step—after hearing their story—is to help them gain some distance from the burden they carry, and through which they often identify themselves. This distancing will provide a clearer vision for courses of action open to them or reveal areas of freedom still available to take a stand toward their conditions.

The first task of the logotherapist is to help the client realize that he is not identical with his symptoms (Lukas, 1979). The resources of the spirit are tapped, its defiant power is awakened so the client sees that fears, obsessions, depressions, feelings of inferiority, and emotional outbursts are not an integral part of who he is but qualities he *has*, which he can modify, and possibly overcome. He learns that he is not the helpless victim of his biological shortcomings, his psychological drives, and his environmental influences; that he is not fated to remain the way he has been, and that there is no situation in which he cannot change unwanted patterns, either in fact or, where this is not possible, in the attitude he takes toward an unchangeable circumstance like the death of a friend or the loss of a limb.

The logotherapist helps clients overcome their feelings of helpless dependence on circumstances "beyond their control" which they sometimes use only to explain their symptoms and their personalities to themselves, and which, in turn, result in a negative feedback that further reinforces their symptoms. And, the logotherapist makes his patients conscious of what they unconsciously know: that they are, first and foremost, human beings with the capacity to find meanings; only secondarily are they individuals who have certain shortcomings which can be overcome and unwanted patterns which can be broken.

To break unwanted patterns, clients have to be led to see themselves from outside, as observers, and not from inside their traps, as victims. How the therapist manages to bring distance between a client and his symptoms is not decisive. It may require some techniques and much improvisation and patience (Fabry et al., eds., 1979, 96-97).

One approach that has worked well for this logotherapist is to invite the client to become the audience to the situation in his life that is problematic. The way this can be accomplished is by saying something along these lines:

"In order to make sure that I (the therapist) understand the full extent of your distress (problem, situation, circumstance, symptom, pain, etc.), let me enter the theater of your life with you. Let's put your situation on the stage of this theater as if it were a play and together we'll watch it unfold. Would you (client) please join me in the audience and describe to me what

is going on on stage. Only you can adequately see and feel and describe the play unfolding before us."

If the client is receptive to this, by becoming the *observer* he begins to *self-distance*; and, by telling the problem from the observer's vantage point, possibilities for optional endings and *changes in attitude* emerge. This is bound to lead to insights and awarenesses that were not available to him while he had totally identified himself with the problem.

The uniquely human quality of self-distancing or detachment enables us to step away from ourselves, look at ourselves from the outside, to oppose ourselves if need be, and even laugh at ourselves at times. This capacity for self-distancing manifests itself in the *defiant power of the human spirit*, the human capacity to take a stand even against oneself. *"I don't have to take every nonsense from myself!"* was one of Dr. Frankl's emphatic phrases.

We see this self-distancing quality perhaps most clearly through the sense of humor. As Frankl points out in *Man's Search for Meaning*, "Humor is another of the soul's weapon in the fight for self-preservation. It is well known that humor, more than anything else in the human makeup, can afford an aloofness and an ability to rise above any situation, even if only for a few seconds" (p. 63). In other words, logotherapy uses humor as a means of distancing self from behaviors and fears. This ability to laugh at oneself and one's situation is a critical element in the healing process for individuals.

Sometimes by stepping away from ourselves and looking at ourselves with a sense of humor we are able to see the ridiculousness of our behavior and fears. Frankl was fond of quoting Gordon Allport's observation: 'A patient who is able to laugh at himself is on the way to recovery' (Fabry et al., *Logotherapy in Action*, 1979, p. 8).

The moment we laugh at our fears, some sense of the fear dissipates. The laughing is not the kind of nervous laughter that comes when we are unsure of what will happen next. This is a genuine humor, a laughing at the exaggerated situation. However, both client and counselor must understand that the target of humor is the ridiculous fears and emotional absurdities, not the client. This is why self-distancing is so important. Clients need assistance in creating distance between self and the behavior or fear before they are able to laugh at or ridicule the behavior or fear (Rice, et al., 2002, Chap. VI).

Self-distancing needs to be understood as a process that will lead from distress to a healthier state of being. It is a tool in the tool kit of the therapist that is particularly useful at the beginning of therapeutic interventions. Once the client has gained some separation from his symptoms or problems, orientation toward meaningful goals must begin. Only then will lasting change, beyond temporary reduction of symptoms, take place.

Paradoxical Intention

The oldest of Frankl's specific treatment techniques, paradoxical intention (PI) was used by him as early as the late 1920s. It entered the annals of psychotherapeutic literature in 1939 (Schweitzer Archiv für Neurologie und Psychiatrie, Vol 43, 26-31), and in a more detailed manner in 1946, in his major work, *Ärztliche Seelsorge* (later translated as *The Doctor and the Soul*).

Paradoxical intention is a concept embedded in the theory of logotherapy that forms the basis of a therapeutic technique. The client who follows PI is encouraged to test alternative constructs which are dramatically different from those which he or she usually employs. The PI attitude is "paradoxical" in that the client intends or wishes for exactly that event which is normally feared.

PI is said to be applicable to psychological phenomena which involve anticipatory anxiety. Thus, for example, the claustrophobiac who anticipates fear of collapsing before entering an elevator, may humorously wish for a total collapse; or, in another example, the insomniac who worries about her ability to fall asleep, may challenge herself and try to stay awake all night. In both cases, the "fear is replaced by a paradoxical wish," so that "the wind is taken out of the sails" of the condition (Frankl, 1969, p. 180).

Research studies have shown paradoxical intention to be effective in the treatment of a number of conditions, such as insomnia (Ascher & Efran, 1978), phobias, and obsessive neuroses (Gerz, 1966). However, as Frankl has wisely cautioned, PI is **not** a technique to be applied indiscriminately. Before attempting to apply PI, the clinician must make sure that the construction system of the client is understood, and that the psychological context of the individual is taken into account (*Analecta Frankliana* 1980, pp. 179-180).

According to Corsini's *Dictionary of Psychology*, logotherapy offers a special technique for the treatment of obsessive-compulsive and phobic neuroses. Although this technique is closely connected with, and predicated on, Frankl's explicit philosophical concepts, it is applied by representatives of other schools, particularly by behavior therapists who have even contributed the experimental proof for the clinical effectiveness of the Frankl PI technique. Paradoxical intention can be defined as having the patient try to do, or wish to have happen, precisely that which he or she fears. The effect is to disarm that anticipatory anxiety which accounts for much of the feedback mechanisms that initiate and perpetuate the neurotic condition (Corsini, 1999, p. 319).

In her logotherapeutic guide to health, *Meaningful Living*, Elisabeth Lukas offers the following advice on "The Application of Paradoxical Intention:"

> Paradoxical intention is essentially a modification of attitudes centered on a symptom. Those who do not know its theoretical base are surprised at the results and suspect something like a magician's trick. But those familiar with its workings realize what a tremendous human resource has been neglected and can now be used.
>
> The application of paradoxical intention is easy and, in almost every case, successful. What is difficult is to create the preconditions for the application which includes a prominent self-distancing. It is absolutely necessary for paradoxical intention that the clients be consciously aware that they are not identified with the feelings dominating them, but that they can choose an attitude toward those feelings and even defy them. The defiant power of the spirit must be sufficiently aroused before paradoxical intention can be applied (Lukas, 1984, p. 73).

James Yoder, in *Meaning in Therapy*, explains that Frankl discovered a way of challenging clients who felt overcome by obsessions, compulsive actions, or fears and phobias; helping them see that while they have fears and compulsions, they are not identical with them. Encouraging a client to join the fear—to even enhance it and revel in it—presents a paradoxical situation which effectively cancels out the fear or phobia. Yoder continues, "One cannot wish or will something to happen and at the same time fear it. Thus, the name *paradoxical intention* comes into play" (p.75). Testing the idea for himself, he recalls an incident that happened in their home which further convinced him of the effectiveness of the PI technique. Yoder tells of how his wife accidentally cut her big toe on a sharp object that had imbedded itself in a rug. Her toe was bleeding profusely. Attempting to check the bleeding with a tissue, she soon saw that more drastic action was needed. Noticing the extent of her injury, he rushed in to help his wife. But she said. "No. James, you can't stand the sight of blood... [you will faint]." He immediately made the decision to try paradoxical intention on himself by 'intending' to faint as he looked at the bleeding toe. He kept repeating the paradoxical intentions of "James, go ahead and faint. You can faint three times here on the kitchen floor. Fall over. Turn whiter than an Indian Ghost plant, etc." while applying first aid. His wife was quite amazed at his coolness and calm nursing abilities. And he was amazed by the effectiveness of the PI technique (Yoder, 1989, p.76).

Subsequently, Dr. Yoder successfully treated clients presenting with a wide variety of symptoms, ranging from a "thumb sucking" little girl who was to be fitted with braces and had to give up her habit before the orthodontist would begin his work on her teeth; "agoraphobia" in a mother of school age children who had not left the house in four years due to her exaggerated fears; and, a number of clients suffering from a variety of obsessive compulsive symptoms.

Socratic Dialogue

Socrates believed that it was the task of the teacher not to pour information into the students, but to elicit from the students what they know intuitively. Frankl believes it is the task of the logotherapist, not to tell clients what the meaning in their life is, but to elicit the wisdom that is hidden within the spirit of each person. One of the basic assumptions of logotherapy is that, in the depth of our spiritual dimension, we know what kind of person we are, what our potentials are, and what is important and meaningful to us.

Frankl discusses the Socratic dialogue as one of the logotherapeutic methods in most of his books. He states that ultimate questions of human existence are on the lips of every man and that these questions are continually confronting the therapist. The awareness of the concrete meaning of one's existence is not at all an abstract one, but is implicit in immediate dedication and devotion. He cautions that it is not necessary to enter into sophisticated debate with the patients or clients because *Logos* is deeper than logic (PE, 57-58).

Therefore, the Socratic dialogue avoids "Why?" questions. They only lead to reasoned-out responses and debates; in other words they engage logic, not necessarily *Logos*. Also avoided are questions that can be answered with "Yes" or "No." Instead, provocative questions are asked centering around: "What," "How," "When," "Who," "Where," "If," etc. These open-ended questions lead to deeper levels of insight.

Paul Welter has well described the Socratic dialogue in the text for the course *Franklian Psychology and Logotherapy* (1995, V/1-2) and has compiled a list of maieutic (midwifing) questions, which help birth latent ideas and initiate the Socratic dialogue. The questions are considered to be "two-legged" questions. One "leg" enters the client's existential paradigm, the other is beyond it and presents a way out of it.

1. *If your whole life had been designed in advance so that you would learn something from it, what would be the lesson you were supposed to have learned?*
2. *As you look back on your life, what were the moments when you were most yourself ?*

3. *What is a goal you would like to accomplish in one month? In six months?*
4. *How do you find courage?*
5. *What is a fear you'd like to be free of?*
6. *What challenge do you have before you right now?*
7. *If you were asked by a child you love to tell the most important thing you have learned in life, what would it be?*
8. *Who was a "cookie" person in your life? (Sid Simon says a cookie person is someone, usually early in our lives, who loved us unconditionally and who gave us time and attention.)*
9. *What is something you'd like to celebrate?*
10. *What is a dream you'd like to have come true someday?*
11. *What is life asking of you at this time, even in all your suffering?*
12. *When do you feel the most renewed?* (Welter, 1995, V/8).

To reiterate, the Socratic dialogue is not an intellectual discussion, not argumentation or manipulation. According to Fabry in *Guideposts to Meaning*, it is rather a teaching/learning that uses experiences—those of the seeker and those of the helper. During the dialogue, the helper elicits ideas and feelings from the seeker by asking questions based on what the seeker says—from "logohints" that the helper finds in the seeker's words. Frankl has turned the Socratic dialogue into a tool that the helper uses most frequently to aid the seeker in the search for meaning. This dialogue brings one in touch with one's healthy core, the spirit, so that one can use its resources (Fabry, 1988, pp. 9-10). Fabry provides examples of how to initiate a Socratic dialogue, and offer some follow-up.

Dialogue with someone who states that he is "in a mess now":

- *You feel that you are in a mess now. Tell me about other times when you were in a mess.*
- *Looking back now, has anything positive come from those situations? Have you learned something from those? Grown? Had experiences you otherwise would not have had?*
- *Did you risk anything to get out of the mess?*
- *How did you get out of it?*
- *Is there anything you can learn from this past experience that can be applied to the current situation?*

Socratic dialogue with someone who procrastinates and whose "will to meaning" and goal orientation needs to be strengthened:

- *What are a few of the things you want to accomplish during the next year? The next three years?*
- *What keeps you from realizing these things?*
- *Pick out the one thing you want most to accomplish.*
- *What would be the first step toward this goal?*
- *What price would you be willing to pay to achieve this goal?*

Socratic dialogue with someone who is down on himself and is looking for direction:

- *Who are your role models?*
- *What do you admire about them? Do you have any qualities they have?*
- *Could you achieve some of the qualities you admire in your models?*
- *What could you do to achieve these qualities, even in a small way?*
- *Does thinking about these qualities give you an inkling about what kind of person you are? About what kind of person you could be?*
- *What are your strong points? Your talents?*
- *What do you need to do to realize your talents?*

- *What are the obstacles to realizing them? How could you overcome these obstacles?* (Fabry, 1998, pp. 11-12)

The above sampling of maieutic questions in the Socratic dialogue was intended only to demonstrate the nature of the questions. They are not intended to be used literally, unless one or the other question happens to be tailor made for the situation at hand.

For many logotherapists the Socratic dialogue that helps to bring the therapeutic process to the core issue of "where is the meaning in your life?" has become the workhorse. As long as we remember that the Socratic dialogue, with its maieutic questions, is innovative and unique to the client and his circumstance or symptoms, fits the personality of the therapist, and is neither interrogative, prying, nor invasive, it will be an excellent tool to use in many situations.

Dereflection

"Dereflection is the therapeutic application of man's will to meaning and his capacity of self-transcendence," states Kurt Kocourek in *Logotherapy in Action*. He explains that by making the will to meaning, rather than the will to pleasure, the central motivation of man, the logotherapist sees man not basically concerned with maintaining or restoring his inner equilibrium by gratifying his drives and instincts, but as directed toward something other than himself, reaching out toward other people and finding meanings to fulfill. The patient is "dereflected" from his disturbance and focused on the task at hand or the partner involved. He quotes Frankl as saying, "Dereflection is intended to counteract compulsive inclination to self-observation. Through paradoxical intention the patient tries to ridicule his symptoms, while he learns to 'ignore' them through dereflection" (Fabry et al., Eds., 1979, p. 85).

A measure of self-observation or self-reflection is normal but under some conditions excessive or "hyper" reflection, and "hyper" intention (WM, pp. 33, 100) can cause disorders in the organism. An example of hyperreflection or excessive self-observation is cited of Frankl's account of a violinist patient who made a great effort to perform as consciously as possible, from putting his violin in place on his shoulder to the most trifling technical details. This resulted in a complete artistic breakdown. The treatment of dereflection was aimed at eliminating his hyperreflection and at restoring the patient's trust in his unconscious, by making him realize how much more musical his unconscious was than his conscious. 'This treatment oriented toward the patient's self-reliance on his unconscious did bring about the release of the artistic creative powers of his unconscious. Dereflection liberated the creative process from the inhibiting effects of any unnecessary reflection.' (Fabry et al. eds., 1979, p. 93)

The following segment on **dereflection** is excerpted from *Viktor Frankl's Logotherapy: Meaning-Centered Interventions* (co-authored with Rice, Pitts, Rogina & Sjolie, 2002), albeit slightly modified. The text points out that dereflection will help us discover meaning in situations where we feel trapped by our own worry about a problem. The problem may be physical, psychological, or existential - that is, a problem of living in the world as it is. Dereflection will not cure a purely physical problem, such as deafness or arthritis, but it will free us from the additional burden that comes from thinking too much about the initial problem.

One difficulty in deciding how to get out of an unwanted situation is the tendency to worry. There is no situation that cannot be made worse by excessive worry. A certain amount of worrying is healthy: it will get us to seek medical or other help. But if we brood on a problem, eventually we will feel as if we are the helpless victim of a problem we cannot solve. It is in situations such as these where dereflection can be applied productively.

Although any problem becomes harder to bear if we think too much about it, it is difficult to decide not to think about a problem. Consider the story about the man who was promised $100 if he would **not** think of a chameleon? Although he had never before thought about this strange creature, now suddenly he could not stop thinking about it. But as soon as he was told to think about an elephant, he stopped thinking about the chameleon. That's the principle behind dereflection. If our problem is caused by too much reflection (what logotherapists call "hyperreflection"), then help comes from *de*reflection by giving it another focus.

Hyperreflecting people take themselves too seriously. Not only do they hyperreflect on their problems, they also "hyperintend"—they pay too much attention to solving their problems with will power. Yet often it is hyperintention that makes it impossible to solve a problem. Dereflection strengthens our capacity for self-transcendence—our ability to reach out beyond self-centeredness toward other people or goals that are meaningful to us.

Unhealthy hyperreflection may focus on a **single symptom** such as a sleep disturbance or a sexual dysfunction. Or it may be a **general attitude toward life**. In either of these situations, hyperreflection is an effort to force a change to occur. In both situations, dereflection can be helpful. Dereflection consists of two parts: a *stop sign* that puts the brakes on pathological hyperreflection, and a *guidepost* that turns the mind to other thoughts. This new direction gradually creates a positive, meaning-oriented (rather than ego-centered) view of the world (Rice, et al., 2002, Chap. VI).

Kocourek in his segment on "Dereflection" in *Logotherapy in Action* reminds us that the logotherapist helps the patient regain his trust in the wisdom of his noetic unconscious–of what often is referred to as "the wisdom of the heart" which also is captured by the wisdom of the language. We speak of "falling" asleep and "falling" in love. Sleep and love cannot be consciously willed, they escape us if we hyperreflect on them or concentrate our intention on them. Only by using the resources of the noetic unconscious, primarily the will to meaning, can we transcend ourselves and reach the objects of our intention, which escape direct assault. Dereflection is a method to achieve this goal (Fabry et al. eds., 1979, pp. 93-94).

Counseling takes place either individually or in group settings. When working with an individual the pastoral psychologist or other helper has the advantage of being able to focus exclusively on one person and listen for clues. While this is preferable, it is not always possible. The Dereflection technique has also been successfully used in the group format as the following example will demonstrate.

The Dereflection Group

A powerful group experience using the method of dereflection was created by Elisabeth Lukas and is described in *Meaning in Suffering* (1986) under the chapter heading, "The Will to Joy As Health Resource" (106-119). Dr. Lukas points out that in most other therapy groups participants talk about their problems. This may worsen their hyperreflection. While retaining the advantages of group therapy (becoming aware that other people have similar problems, becoming less inhibited by participating in the group format, and hearing others' ideas about how they solve their problems), she also introduces positive aspects into her therapy groups by focusing on the good in life. She calls her groups "dereflection groups" (p.109).

The safe group setting serves as a forum where attitudes shift rather rapidly from negative self-centered observations to positive self-transcending ones. Instead of focusing on "what's wrong," group members are to state, instead, "what's right." The sessions are not allowed to deteriorate into complaining about fate, victimhood, blaming, etc. Her axiom is, *Why do you stand in the Garden of Life and water the weeds instead of the flowers?* Attention is given to what is positive, joyful, uplifting. Group members learn to focus on worthwhile attainable goals, instead of past failures (Lukas, 1986, pp. 106-109).

Which Technique Do I Use?

The question of technique often looms prominently when counselors are faced with problems brought before them. Frankl speaks to this topic in *Psychotherapy and Existentialism*, where he reminds us that the psychotherapeutic process consists of a continuous chain of improvisations; and, that the extent to which psychotherapy can be taught and learned has frequently been questioned. In addition, one must bear in mind that the infinite diversity of patients precludes the possibility of extrapolating from one patient to another. Thus, the psychotherapist is always faced with the seemingly impossible twofold task of considering the uniqueness of each person, as well as the uniqueness of the life situation with which each person has to cope. Nevertheless, it is precisely this *individuation* and *improvisation* which must be taught and must be learned (1985, p. 141). Frankl continues:

> The choice of an appropriate treatment method to be applied in any concrete case depends not only upon the *individuality* of the patient involved but also upon the *personality* of the therapist. The difficulty of the problem lies in the fact that the last two factors must be considered as

> "unknowns," at least initially. To illustrate this point, I frequently tell my students that the choice of the therapeutic method to be used in a specific situation may be compared to the following algebraic equation; $\psi = x + y$, wherein ψ is the therapeutic method, x represents the individuality of the patient, and y stands for the physician involved (1985, PE, pp.140-141).

This equation highlights the fact that the crucial agency in psychotherapy is not so much the method as the relationship. In view of the above, no method or technique can claim to be "the best." Like a good tool, the technique must fit the hand that yields the tool; and, the tool must be appropriate for the task at hand. However, Frankl strongly admonishes that the therapist must beware of interpreting his role as a mere technician. This would amount to reducing the client or patient to a mere human machine.

The entire structure of logotherapy rests on the premise that the human being, as a spiritual being, has to be treated in his ontological entirety—body, psyche and spirit. Only when the individuality of the client and the personality of the counselor are seen in that light, will the therapeutic process take on human elements of individualization and improvisation, and lead to deeply meaningful therapeutic encounters that can bring about healing and growth.

Please note: The founder of the Viktor Frankl Institute of Logotherapy, Joseph Fabry, adds this note of caution:

> If a problem has physical causes, medical and pharmaceutical help must be sought. Most difficulties discussed here have psychological origins and can be helped [by methods of logotherapy]. But a medical diagnosis is recommended before a therapy plan is entered (Fabry, 1988, pp. 31-32).

VII

EXAMPLES of LOGOTHERAPEUTIC INTERVENTIONS

Application of Logotherapy in Inescapable Suffering

The holistic philosophy of an integrated human being centered in a spiritual core, as postulated by Viktor Frankl, is nearly universally acceptable. It appeals not only to the religiously inclined, but also to secular humanists, agnostics, even atheists. The perennial wisdom of Frankl's philosophy is inclusive, existential (being concerned with the "here and now" of existence), and future oriented. It is firmly grounded in realism - even pragmatism. It advocates action in areas where action is needed, seeks to find meaning in suffering where cure is no longer possible, and looks to the future with hope.

Frankl has placed all experiences arising from our human condition into five general areas. These common areas of experience are filled with meaning potential and provide occasions for growth. They are perceived as follows:

- The Meaning of Life
- The Meaning of Death
- The Meaning of Suffering
- The Meaning of Work
- The Meaning of Love (1985, DS, pp. 25-175).

According to logotherapy it is intrinsic to human nature to want to find meaning in these above areas of human existence. None of us is exempt from reflecting on the above listed manifests

APPLICATION OF LOGOTHERAPY
in Key Areas of Human Suffering:

PEOPLE IN DESPONDENCY

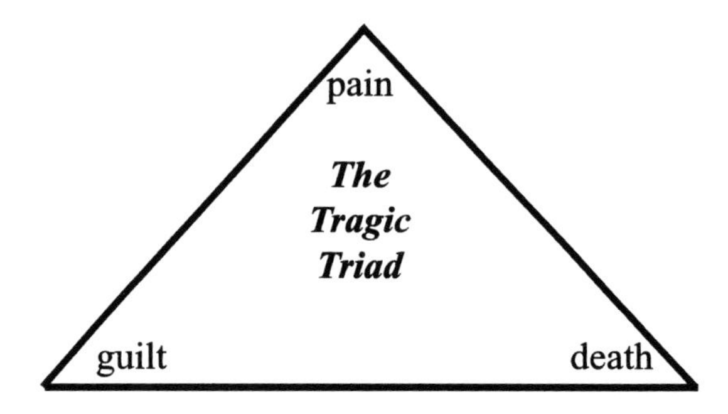

PEOPLE IN DESPAIR

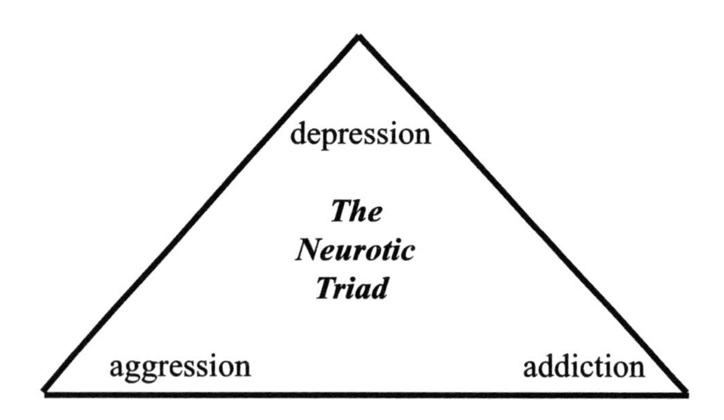

PEOPLE IN DOUBT AND CONFUSION

Access to the noetic dimension is blocked

Existential Vacuum

Fig. 7

of human life. Most of the time, we can handle the lessons life brings to us. Occasionally, too much happens too quickly, or we are hurt too deeply and we need to seek help. Then we join the long lines of the despondent, despairing, doubting and confused, who seek out the services of those who have the compassion to hear us and the wisdom to guide us.

The long roster of common problems listed in Chapter III, which are brought before helpers dealing in pastoral psychology and related fields, can readily be absorbed into the five divisions dealing with the *Meaning of Life, Death, Suffering, Work, and Love.* Frankl has postulated that the problems associated with these key areas of human life also have roots in common; that there are underlying dynamics which drive most, if not all, human problems. They can be grouped into three basic categories. These driving forces of most of our problems are: **despondency, despair, doubt and confusion**, and combinations thereof. He delineated how certain problems group around each of these dynamics or characteristic energies.

The preceding diagram (Fig. 7) offers an overview of key areas "homo patiens" or the suffering human being is likely to encounter in the course of life. It identifies various dynamics that are the underlying driving force in each area of human suffering. The myriad of presenting symptoms or problems, which brings clients to seek help, may be found primarily in one category or another, but can also present in combination of one or more dynamics arising from the search for meaning in Life, Death, Suffering, Work, or Love.

People experiencing **despondency** are often caught in a ***tragic triad***: they are pained, guilty, or grieving. They may feel helpless and overwhelmed by fate. Conditions of the tragic triad are an inescapable part of human existence.

People in **despair** will tend to struggle with the ***neurotic triad*** of depression, aggression, and addiction. It may help to recognize that even though the outer manifestations appear vastly different, the underlying energy that drives this triad is the same—it is despair. It points to noogenic distress.

People in **doubt and confusion** are plagued by an ***existential vacuum***, an inner emptiness or void that presents as the boredom of a meaningless existence. They may drift into conformity and apathy. Their avenues to finding meaning appear blocked because access to their noetic energies is obstructed.

To explicate how logotherapy has been effectively practiced in these key areas, phenomenological material in the form of case presentations will be included in this chapter, following the description of each underlying dynamic.

The Tragic Triad: People in Despondency

The question is asked in *Man's Search for Meaning*, "How is it possible to say yes to life in spite of the 'tragic triad'... a triad which consists of those aspects of human existence which may be circumscribed by: (1) pain; (2) guilt; and (3) death." (Frankl, 1985, p. 161). These are the aspects of life none of us can escape. They can lead to despondency, yet they have their role to play.

In the same breath Frankl speaks of a *tragic optimism*, an optimism in the face of tragedy inherent in the human condition, and in view of human potential, which—at its best—allows for transformation. Here are some of the possible outcomes derived from pain, guilt, and death if the *tragic triad* is viewed as life's taskmaster that provides the means to turn despondency into tragic optimism:

1) **Pain**: turning suffering into a human achievement and accomplishment.

2) **Guilt**: deriving from guilt the opportunity to change oneself for the better.
3) **Death**: deriving from life's transitoriness an incentive to take responsible action.

It must be kept in mind, however, that this *tragic optimism* for transformation cannot be commanded or ordered. Frankl cautions:

> One cannot even force oneself to be optimistic indiscriminately, against all odds, against all hope. And what is true for hope is also true for the other two components of [that] triad inasmuch as faith and love cannot be commanded or ordered either (Frankl, 1985, MSM p.162).

Just as happiness cannot be pursued directly, it must ensue, so it is with the search for meaning. Meaning will dawn upon us as we actualize the meaning potential inherent in the tragic triad. We must have faith that life presents us with opportunities for growth that lie dormant in suffering–be it pain, guilt, or death. Only then can we transmute the conditions confronting us through the optimism of faith, hope, and love into the triumph of real human inner achievement.

Pain

No one on the planet is a stranger to pain. It wears many guises. There is the *physical pain* we are all subject to from the pain of teething to the pain experienced in acute or chronic illness. There is the *psychological pain* born of the disappointments of life; the pain of interpersonal conflicts; betrayal of trust; the pain of goals not reached; anguish of loneliness; the agony of victimization; the loss of meaningful work. There is also *spiritual pain* that stalks us in the form of doubts and loss of faith; struggles in our prayer life or communication with God; spiritual confusion and indifference, and the loss of vision and hope.

Guilt

Guilt was described by Dr. Lukas in a lecture as a complex subject that comes under the heading of overcoming failure. Here we enter the realm of our personal past, for any current happening is still in the stage of development and cannot be called a failure before it has reached a conclusion. By failure is meant failure for which we are responsible. Failures for which we are not responsible belong in the category of unavoidable suffering.

Regarding failures for which we are responsible, the gods are not very merciful: they rarely cover these failures with total oblivion, rather they let a little tip show, which functions as "guilty conscience." This does not necessarily mean that there is emotional damage. On the contrary, it might even lead to spiritual maturity. In logotherapy, guilt is looked upon as an opportunity to change, as an appeal to abandon old patterns and make new and better decisions (Lukas, 1989).

A word on "collective guilt" seems to be appropriate here. In an article on collective guilt, featured in the *International Forum for Logotherapy*, Elisabeth Lukas, a foremost student of Frankl, reiterates how Dr. Frankl, a survivor of four concentration camps, has spoken out all his life against the theory of the collective guilt of the German people. Lukas states that Frankl gave a now famous speech in which he urged that a Jew must go and confirm that there were both kinds of people under the Nazi regime, decent people and unprincipled people, and that it would be unjust to condemn them all, lock, stock, and barrel. No Aryan has the authorization, so to speak, to proclaim this truth. An Aryan would be accused of trying to smooth over the atrocities of his race. No, a Jew who has suffered cruelly under the Aryan henchmen must go and confirm this. Then the next generation will understand that there are only two "races" of human beings on earth, namely the decent and the unprincipled, and these are present in all peoples and cultures, societies, and nations (Lukas *IFL*, Vol 15, #2 1992, p. 96).

Death

Logotherapy, contrary to the general attitude of our culture, has given much attention to death. Facing the issue of death means becoming aware of our *transitoriness*. We are dealing with the question of how to handle our knowledge that we are mortal, living for a time on a given planet, the Earth.

Logotherapy once again relies on its *optimism* and points out that nothing can take away the valuable acts we have done, which are irretrievably anchored in our past. Every task we have fulfilled, every happy experience, every suffering courageously borne, every guilt redeemed in a mature manner – all these things have become part of the eternity of the past, the essence of our being, the quality of our life, our identity. None of this can be taken away from us, even long after we have returned to dust.

What is past still remains as it was; nothing can wipe it out. Frankl often remarked, "Thinking of something cannot make it happen; by the same token, no longer thinking of something cannot destroy it." It remains. Whether the level of its quality makes any difference, is a question that we can only answer through faith. But our deep longing for salvation and our existentially rooted search for meaning indicates that what has remained of each of us in our past does matter. It becomes our monument (Lukas, 1989).

Logotherapy focuses less on the origin of a given cause of suffering and more on the overcoming of it. It recognizes that pain, guilt, death are an unalterable reality of human existence, and must be borne. Logotherapy attempts to help the client to get in touch with his reservoir of strengths within, and to apply the power of the human spirit to overcome the distress which follows in the wake of suffering in any category. It patiently supports the sufferer without fostering dependency upon the therapist; above all, it is non-judgmental and treats each person with dignity and respect.

An example of one person's victory in dealing with elements of the **tragic triad**, namely *pain, guilt,* and *death* (in this case irrevocable loss), is offered here to demonstrate the logotherapeutic process.

The case of Lucy (fictitious name)

I came upon Lucy during the holidays at an open-house party. She sat in a dark room, all alone, crying. Although I had met her before as a friend of the hostess, I had felt Lucy would be hard to get to know because she seemed to have an armor of protective coating about her. Now her heart-rending sobs drew me to her. When I asked, "Lucy, what is it?" she put me off by saying, " I can't talk about it!" Nevertheless, I felt I ought to stay with her. As it turned out I would do the most intensive logotherapy I had ever done - while a party was in progress downstairs.

After sitting with her quietly for a while, I began a Socratic Dialogue by saying, "Lucy, you seem so sad, so despondent ... I wonder, what could have caused you such pain?" Bit by bit, between sobs and tears, Lucy haltingly told me about the cause of her anguish, her shame, and guilt.

As a young girl she had been a devout Catholic and wanted to become a nun. She entered the convent after high school. Her family was glad. After five years in the novitiate she found she did not fit, nor did it give her the peace and joy she had hoped for. Coming out of the convent was traumatic; especially, since she didn't have any marketable skills to support herself. Going back home was out of the question. She eked out a living through door-to-door sales.

In time, she met a man who she thought was "the love of her life." They lived together. Lucy had been looking forward to a future with him, had been dreaming of marriage and family. When she found she was pregnant, he couldn't face the responsibility. He not only abandoned her, but turned to another woman; as Lucy put it, "He ran away with his mistress."

She was shocked to the core, destitute, and ill. Her family treated her as "the scarlet woman" who brought nothing but disgrace upon them. They hid her existence (and her pregnancy) as much as possible. "As the time of birth approached I went to a Catholic hospital," she said, "where they gave medical assistance to girls like me, but kept me in a separate unit in total isolation without any relief for pain during three long days in labor. No one came to visit me... I was so scared... My body was racked with contractions that went on and on... Worst of all, I felt like a moral leper and a social outcast."

Following the difficult delivery she placed the baby, a little boy, for adoption - wanting a better life for him than she was able to offer. She left the hospital and tried to pick up the pieces of her shattered life. At first she plotted to kill the father of her child and his mistress. Gradually the grief over the loss of her baby consumed all energy for revenge.

"The holidays are the worst time for me... second only to his birthday," sighed Lucy. "Mothers have so much fun getting Christmas gifts for their children. I can't even tell anyone that I had a child... Never even made Christmas cookies for him..."

Here I began to probe in the hope of effecting an attitudinal change: "Have you ever made a birthday cake to commemorate the occasion?"

Lucy: "A b... birth... birthday cake? I never thought of it. But I look at his birth certificate just to acknowledge that he exists! No one ever saw it. No one ever wanted to see it." She cries uncontrollably.

Ann: "Does he have a name?"

Lucy: "I named him George, little George."

Ann: "Lucy, how old will little George be on his next birthday?"

Lucy: "He'll be 18. Why... he's nearly grown."

Ann: "Lucy, how would you like to plan a birthday party for George? A kind of "Coming of Age Party" where you tell him everything that's in your heart concerning him?"

Lucy: "Who would come?"

Ann: "I'd be honored to receive an invitation to such a party."

Lucy: "You would? You don't think I'm a degenerate, totally worthless woman?"

Ann: "No, Lucy!" Resolutely I shake my head.

Then I witnessed the most cathartic experience I had ever seen as Lucy released years and years of pent-up grief, anguish, repressed emotions over the loss of a child she loved and couldn't acknowledge publicly. Her deep painful secret was out and she learned that her worst fear, the fear that she would be judged and condemned, had been unfounded.

Spent from violent sobbing she continued to cry softly while I talked to her gently about her deep love for her child. I pointed out her courage in living through the pregnancy after she had been abandoned.

Lucy: "That's right! I still could have had an abortion. In 20 minutes that life would have been snuffed out. My conscience wouldn't let me do that. Something made me carry him to term" [in spite of illness and complications of pregnancy].

I told her that she made a self-transcending choice in spite of great obstacles and that the time for celebrating that choice had come; time for acknowledging the defiant power of the spirit that had brought her through this.

Lucy: "Yes... You know, after I found better work, mostly clerical, I went to night school. Eventually I earned a teaching certificate. But I stayed away from schools in fear. What if one of the kids turned out to be George?"

Since I know of Lucy's religious background, we talked about the sustaining assistance of God (grace) operative in her life, how it could help her transform this fear into anticipatory excitement.

She began to see herself as a woman of courage who had suffered much and had grown strong. A lavage of the soul or cleansing seems to have occurred - her shame and guilt lifted. She felt absolved, freed from the burden of the past.

Post-Notes: Following the initial cathartic experience Lucy entered therapy. During treatment, the **Socratic dialogue** figured prominently in her sessions. At times she needed to **self-distance** in order to see the panorama of her life more clearly. Opportunities for **paradoxical intention** presented themselves occasionally, but **logotherapeutic dereflection** was frequently necessary to dislodge her from brooding on the past. Beyond that, Lucy's therapeutic process demanded **individuation and improvisation** (i.e., the birthday party where George's existence was acknowledged and celebrated).

The healing process demanded patience from the therapist and a great deal of courage from Lucy as she faced her pain, guilt, and loss. In the end, she saw that she had developed strengths from her tribulations. She found meaning in her past, and hope for the future. Eventually she even found the courage to seek employment as a teacher. In her position as art teacher, she encountered young people of all ages. When she was asked in a later visit, "Lucy, what if one of the kids turns out to be George?" Her eager reply was, "I'd want to be the best teacher he ever had!" At that point I knew that her transformed self-image was firmly in place and therapy could be terminated, yet the door left open in case she wanted to return for occasional follow-up sessions.

The Neurotic Triad: People in Despair

In his thirty-second and last book, *Man's Search for Ultimate Meaning*, published in 1997 just weeks before his death, Frankl writes, "Among the world wide effects is what one might call the **mass neurotic triad**, which consists of depression, addiction, and aggression." (p. 99). The underlying energy of **despair**, the driving force of the neurotic triad, can be viewed as summarized by Paul Welter (1995, IX-2):

1) **Depression**: Depressed persons who are *desperate* may attempt suicide. Suicide is the crispest statement of *despair* and lack of meaning.
2) **Addiction**: Addicts' *despair* shows in their attempts to numb themselves or seek a thrill with some substance or behavior.
3) **Aggression**: Aggressive persons, in their *despair*, turn to trying to control others by violence.

Instead of addressing each of the problem areas associated with the **neurotic triad**, namely *depression*, *addiction*, and *aggression* separately, the focus will be on the underlying **despair** instead.

Furthermore, each of the three disorders may involve **violence**. The third disorder, *aggression*, does so by definition. But *depression* may involve violence to oneself, as in suicide; and, *addiction* often worsens any violent behavior that is present. For example, many alcoholics are often more aggressive when they drink. Violence has been viewed as a *noogenic neurosis* or disturbance due to moral conflicts or from spiritual problems (Frankl, 1963/1977, p. 160).

Many therapies work with the remediation of violent behavior. Logotherapy is uniquely able (in the person who has high cognitive function still) to go to the root cause of violent behavior, namely despair. (Verbal therapy alone is NOT intended for those who must be restrained for their own or for the protection of others.)

A model for treating violent behavior, where logotherapy figures prominently, was developed by Julius Rogina, Ph.D., a clinical psychologist and logotherapist, whose work necessitated something beyond the purely psychological interventions of behavioral modification. A synopsis of the Rogina five stage model for treating violent behavior as presented in *Viktor Frankl's Logotherapeutic Model of Mental Health* (Graber, Rogina, 2000, Chap. VIII), follows:

The Rogina Model for Treating Violent Behavior (VCCFM)

Stage I: Violent behaviors and awareness of their perpetration:

Work with client and family on creating a sense of discomfort, disturbing one's conscience.

Develop therapeutic relationships.

Address substance abuse issues.

Logotherapy: Hyper-reflection on violent behaviors [to bring their perpetration to awareness and get beyond denial].

Stage II: Confrontation:

Direct intervention.

Ego-strengthening.

Safe remembering of specific violent behaviors.

Logotherapy: Self-transcendence; Value clarification with honesty and courage.

Stage III: Confession:

Naming violent behaviors, continue ego-strengthening. Empowerment for "confessing" to self and others specific violent behaviors.

Connecting sensory, visual, behavioral, motoric, affective, cognitive, spiritual aspects of violence.

Logotherapy: Noetic dimension accessing, values confrontation.

Stage IV: **F**orgiveness:

Client asks for forgiveness of the ones being hurt or self that has been violated. Ego-strengthening, acceptance, ratification, working through noetic material.

"Letting go"—Stories to enforce sense of forgiveness. Ongoing processing of traumatic behaviors.

Future identity integration. Personality reintegration as forgiven and accepted.

Logotherapy: Dereflection. Future focusing on meaningful goals.

Stage V: **M**eaningful living behaviors:

Name specific meaningful, noetically anchored behaviors.

[Establish] Guideposts to responsibility.

[Find] Guideposts to uniqueness.

Modification of attitudes.

Acceptance and ongoing reconciliation of the experience of opposites.

Logotherapy: Living for... [someone or something]

Noetic unfolding.

As stated earlier, violence tends to be an attendant factor in the **neurotic triad** consisting of *depression, addiction,* and *aggression* Dr. Rogina's VCCFM Model treats not only the behavior, but seeks to orient the client to the noetic dimension and ongoing spiritual growth.

When treating conditions in the ***neurotic triad***, the etiology of *underlying despair* needs to be addressed, not just the presenting symptoms, in order to bring about lasting change. The client needs to be helped to choose a life with meaning that will replace the existing despair, which points to noogenic distress or a "troubled spirit."

An example (from the author's files) of a person experiencing despair due to an unalterable fate, which lead to suicidal ideations, follows. It demonstrates how despair lifts when a meaningful goal to pursue is found.

Katie's Despair

Katie, an 18 year old high school senior, a patient in the Burn Unit of a local hospital, was referred by her plastic surgeon upon discharge. Katie had suffered deep and superficial 2nd degree burns over most of her body as a toddler when she was accidentally scalded. Hypertrophic scarring resulted. As she grew in size, numerous surgeries were necessary to expand the skin to provide greater ease of movement.

The most recent surgery was timed so she could use her Christmas break to recuperate. On discharge, the plastic surgeon informed her that further surgeries will not be necessary since she had now reached adult height.

Upon hearing this Katie asked horrified, "What about the scars?"

He gently tried to explain to her that nothing further can be done surgically about the remaining scars.

As the implications of this prognosis dawned upon her, Katie stated emphatically, "If this is what I'm going to look like for the rest of my life, then I don't want to live!"

At this point, the plastic surgeon, who had treated this girl since childhood and knew her well, contacted the pastoral counselor and asked for an immediate appointment. It was pointed out to him that it may not be in the patient's best interest to discharge her from the hospital when she is telling him plainly, "I don't want to live!"

He explained that he would prefer, at this stage, not to send her to the psychiatric ward for observation because SHE would interpret the interven-

tion as, "Not only am I disfigured, but now HE thinks I'm crazy!" That would only compound the problem. He continued, "Besides, it's Christmas Eve. Spending Christmas in the hospital is not going to lift her spirit either. Will you see her right away if I send her over? I would like your impression on the seriousness of her threat."

Shortly thereafter the patient arrived at the office, accompanied by her parents. After the initial introductions, I took Katie to the counseling room to get her own version of what was happening. She told me that although the trauma of the scalding accident had occurred in early childhood, until today she had lived in the hope that eventually all the painful treatments she had been undergoing would restore her to having "normal looking skin." Now she learned that this would not happen. All her hopes for a "normal" life had been dashed. No, she did not want to live if she was going to look like this forever.

Obviously Katie was a strong-willed girl; there was no point in trying to dissuade her. So I opted to buy a little time and asked her if there was anything she wanted or needed to do yet before she killed herself.

She pondered that question and said, "Yes! I made and wrapped all my Christmas presents for my family and friends early this year because I knew I would go to the hospital. I want to give everyone their gifts first."

Therapist (with an inaudible sigh of relief): "Then you are not going to do anything drastic today?"

Katie: "No!"

Therapist: "Tomorrow?"

Katie: "Not on Christmas!"

Therapist: "The day after?"

Katie: "Maybe..."

Therapist: "Before you do, Katie, would you come back to see me one more time?"

Katie: "I could do that."

Therapist: "Good. Is that a promise?"

Katie: "Yes!"

Therapist: "Thank you! Then, let's say good-bye for today and start getting ready for Christmas. Hope everyone will like your presents, Katie. I will look forward to seeing you the day after Christmas. Let's go now and see when your parents can bring you back for a follow-up appointment."

This was our initial meeting. I felt reasonably sure that it was safe to let her go for the time being, but wondered privately about her long-term prognosis. At eighteen, when looks are so important to girls, she had to face her unalterable fate that eradication of hypertrophic scarring was not possible at our present state of medical knowledge.

Katie kept her word and with the support of her parents returned for all her subsequent appointments. Coming to terms with her loss of hope to look "normal" (her frequent term), free from disfiguring scars was difficult for her. When I asked her one day, "Katie, what hurts you the most?", her irate answer was, "People don't see who you are, they just notice what you look like!"

"If that's what's important (meaningful) to you, you can do something about showing people who you are," was my challenge to Katie.

Shortly after this conversation, Katie volunteered to tutor a little boy in grade school who had just arrived in this country and didn't speak English. His plight moved her deeply and stirred her out of her self-absorption. She told of her joy of being met by him eagerly every day. He did not seem to notice her scars. He excitedly wanted to practice his new vocabulary with her. She was eager to teach him more. It became an adventure for both of them. The more this spirited young lady could express "who she was," the less preoccupied she became with "what she looked like."

One day, Katie had this insight to share: "I've been pondering the old saying about the glass being half-full or half-empty. It seems to me, it doesn't really matter if it's half-full or half-empty, as long as you get into the water and swim."

I took this to be Katie's metaphor for saying, "I want to live!" and replied, "Katie, your insight is profound! In which direction are you going to swim in life?" She responded, "I want to be a teacher; I learned that from little Ramon." Her self-transcending act of volunteering to tutor not only helped lift her out of her despair, but also gave her a direction for her future, which she did not have before.

When I asked Katie for permission to use her story for inclusion in this presentation, there was a long pause. Then she said, ***"I'd be proud to know that people will hear it. Maybe it will encourage someone else, who is in despair, to hang on to life."***

Post-Notes: The application of methods of logotherapy in this case proceeded as follows:

Initially, when addressing Katie's threat of suicide, an incentive had to be found immediately that would, at least, postpone her intention to carry out her threat. Only she could supply such a compelling reason. **Dereflection** was initiated to focus away from self-destruction toward a meaningful short-term goal to fulfill (Christmas presents to give to family and friends).

A **Socratic dialogue** was employed to elicit what was meaningful and important enough to her to postpone her suicidal projection. Temporary **self-distancing** from her suicidal ideation was a necessary element. Attempts at dissuasion would only have added fuel to the fire in this strong-willed girl.

Then came the long slow process of changing her attitude from despairing about having to live with her scars to wanting to live in spite of them. The defiant power of her spirit was a major ally in this process. Katie's despair had more of an aggressive quality than a depressed victim stance. Her aggression was turned toward self.

This girl needed to be challenged to something greater than plotting her self-destruction. (Show the world who you are!)

Occasionally we played with **paradoxical intention**, particularly when transforming her self-image from self-rejection to self-acceptance. When she could exaggerate her perception of her scars to the point of absurdity, spontaneous laughter disarmed her anxiety and eased her pain.

The real turning point came when she found an outlet for her considerable energy that was self-transcending and rewarding (tutoring little Ramon). This experience reconnected her with her will to live; and, it gave her direction for her future. She took action on that decision by applying for admission to a teacher's college, thus reaching for a long-term, meaningful goal.

Existential Vacuum: People in Doubt and Confusion

Today more choices are available to us than have been available to any generation before now. We can choose not only where to live, but also how to live. We can choose our career, our partner, to have children or not to have children. All those choices bring with them a degree of uncertainty not experienced in times past when family, church, and state had a more decisive influence on our thinking and acting. As a consequence, we deal with more **self-doubt** and **confusion** than previous generations.

In our uncertainty we often vacillate in our decisions, wondering whether they are right or wrong, and sometimes we are paralyzed into a state of indecision. Then it becomes tempting to conform to societal pressures around us, and to give up our responsibility for making choices that are based on our personal values—choices that are authentic and meaningful. When we allow that influence to take over, we have set the stage for an inauthentic life.

As we drift farther and farther from our authentic self, our noetic core, we are buffeted by the waves of opinions about us, we tend to become inconsistent and incongruent, and our loyalties may shift like changes in the weather. Gradually we may lose the capacity to decide on our own behalf. This is fertile soil in which the existential vacuum or inner emptiness can flourish.

A related plight to the state of doubt is the quandary of **ambivalence** or self-contradiction. Here we experience confusion due to contradictory thoughts and emotions toward the same person or situation at the same time. Or we may experience ambivalence between our vision or dream for life and the reality confronting us. We are beset by uncertainty, drifting between opposing polarities, without a firm center. This very drifting about may consume most of our time and energy that could be put to better use if decisiveness and goal orientation were present.

We can help the doubtful, confused, and the ambivalent person, first of all, by strengthening their "Will to Meaning." Exploring available choices and their potential consequences will serve to enlarge the person's perspective so that the meaning potential of each choice can be seen more clearly. The vacillating person needs to learn to understand that there are "ups" and "downs" on every seesaw or that there is light and shadow in everything. Learning to prefer one over the other is the beginning of taking a stand. Learning to listen for that clear "yes" or "no" from within becomes the challenge and the "meaning of the moment." With practice, making choices–meaningful and authentic choices–becomes as habitual as ambivalence or confusion once were (Frankl, lecture, 1985).

Our world is changing fast. Mechanical servants (machines and computers) are doing much of the work humans used to perform. This leaves us unoccupied, and we may start to wonder about our place in the scheme of things and the meaning of life. Frankl calls this lack of meaning "the collective neurosis of our times." When we see no meaning to life, we feel empty. This state is called by logotherapy the *existential vacuum*. As the name so well describes, we live in a vacuum; we feel apathetic, listless, and have no initiative. It affects social behavior and reflects on family life. It makes us feel useless, not an essential part of society.

Many people, especially the young, try to fill this vacuum with violence, drugs, food, and sex. For them life seems to have no meaning. Traditions that provided stability and anchoring of people in society are vanishing, and values are changing rapidly. Added to this is the high mobility of our society that makes it difficult to establish roots. Consequently, especially those in an identity crisis will suffer this inner void.

The existential vacuum is in itself not a pathological state. It should be seen as a sign, calling to our attention, that access to the noetic dimension is blocked. Symptoms of the existential vacuum manifest as: doubt, inner emptiness, boredom, lack of initiative, apathy, nameless dread, conformism, fatalistic thinking, ambivalence, and a sense that existence is meaningless.

Many of us have experienced some of these thoughts and feelings that are characteristic of the existential vacuum sometime during our lives, particularly during transitional phases. However, most of us manage to find meaning for our lives again, sooner or later. The existential vacuum only becomes pathological when it remains a chronic state, slowly leading to *existential frustration* and finally to *noogenic neurosis*. Therefore, if no meaning can be found, it leads to psychic and somatic symptoms. Depression sets in and anxiety overwhelms the person.

The way out is by finding meaning either in creativity (giving something to the world), experiencing something or encountering someone (receiving something from the world in relationship to it or with others), or by changing our attitudes when faced with an unalterable situation (Frankl, 1988, WM, 83-98).

A case study from the author's files will serve as an example of someone experiencing an existential vacuum and overcoming it in his inimitable way:

The Case of Fr. Joseph (pseudonym)

During a professional seminar I was approached by a colleague who was seeking help for one of his clients. His client was a Catholic order priest who had suffered a heart attack. Although the client was making a good recovery medically, he was despondent - going through the motions of living without being alive. His community was concerned and sought help for his psychological malaise.

My colleague had tried numerous interventions to no avail. Discouraged, he asked me if I would see his priest client, hoping that logotherapy could make a difference here. I hesitated... wondering whether a Catholic priest would want to come to a non-Catholic church to talk with a woman pastoral counselor? But I agreed to see him, if the client were receptive to this referral. Apparently there was no objection and an appointment was made.

When I met Fr. Joseph in my church office, my first impression was, 'Here is a noble soul–caught in an existential vacuum.' He seemed to be at ease and readily told me how he began his religious formation at the pre-seminary level at age fourteen. He liked the high ideals which his religious order espoused. He entered the religious life as a very young man and, in time, became a priest. For more than four decades he performed the duties assigned to him faithfully and unquestioningly. Then his heart stopped.

Since his heart attack, he had been reviewing his life and questioning the value of some of the rules he had lived by; he had his doubts and was confused about what he believed; his spiritual life seemed to be in limbo. The strongest discernible emotion was fear - he feared another heart attack.

I asked him if having another heart attack was his greatest fear. He answered, "No, not the heart attack, per se. But if that were the end, I'd stand there before God with my emptiness, with no return on His talents he had entrusted to me. "

When I tried to point out his long years of faithful service as a priest, he brushed it aside, saying firmly, "I did my duty!" Then I asked him what specific talent he felt he had been given by God that could yet be increased?

A smile spread slowly across his face. Shyly he said, "Sometimes I fancied myself a painter... Oh, I've had art classes here and there, but there has never been enough time to devote to painting. "

I suggested that perhaps now, while he was convalescing, there could be time for painting. He nodded thoughtfully, saying, "Yes, I could take my easel and move into our hermitage for awhile and just paint. Yes.... I'd like that!"

At last, I detected a spark of aliveness returning with the anticipation of a personally meaningful creative endeavor ahead. Noodynamic tension was being activated. Here was something freely chosen that he wanted to do; something that was not subject to compliance with extrinsic rules, but had intrinsic value for him.

For several months Fr. Joseph painted. Off and on, when he was in town, he came to see me. A transformative change was observable in him. On his last visit he described his experience while painting in this way: "You know, as a member of a religious order, prayer has played an important role in my life. I've prayed with people, I've prayed for people. Prayer has been my way of communicating with God and others. But this is different! When I'm totally immersed in painting, it's beyond communicating: It's like being in total communion with my Creator and his entire creation. Ah..., if this is what heaven is like, I'm ready. "

Father was late for his next scheduled appointment, which was very uncharacteristic for him. After waiting for some time, 1 called to see if he was on his way. A reluctant voice on the telephone told me, "No, he is not. Fr. Joseph will not be coming any more... He died of a massive heart attack yesterday. "

Post-Notes: In the foregoing example we see a person suffering an inner emptiness or void, indulging in fatalistic thinking and experiencing existential dread (fearing another heart attack). In his psychological malaise he is exhibiting a lack of initiative and general apathy. Conformity to unexamined values eventually led to a state of **existential vacuum**.

Logotherapy teaches that the existential vacuum is NOT a disease in and of itself, but a symptom calling attention to the fact that access to the noetic dimension is somehow blocked and vital energies are not available.

When this symptom is recognized, the client must be helped to reach from his present state of emptiness and despondency to his vision of who he may yet become. ("Sometimes I fancy myself a painter.") In the case of Fr. Joseph, this was accomplished through **creative activity**, one of the three avenues to finding meaning.

In the end, not only his short term goal of getting past his inner void that manifested symptomatically as depression and apathy (going through the motions of living without being alive) but also his life-long goal of "communion with God and all His creation" was achieved—in this client's unique way.

 cs

A Note of Caution

As a psychotherapeutic application, logotherapy can serve as a primary intervention in the areas described. Since logotherapy engages the client intellectually, emotionally, and spiritually, it is necessary that the client be able to actively participate in the process. This mandates a fairly high level of cognitive functioning. In cases of clinical pathology, which require medical and pharmacological treatment, logotherapy may serve as an adjunct therapy or after the acute pathology has been stabilized. Beyond referring the client for treatment to those who are credentialed and competent to provide it, acute mental illness is not an area the pastoral psychologist or counselor would address.

VIII

OF SPECIAL INTEREST to PASTORAL CAREGIVERS

Provide Comfort Where Cure is Not Possible

Psychotherapy exists to treat and, hopefully, heal the suffering and afflicted. Yet, so many concerns brought before pastoral caregivers are beyond a "cure." When that is the case, the words of the prophet Isaiah, *"Comfort ye, comfort ye my people,"* (Isaiah 40:1) must be heeded.

Frankl speaks to this (*The Doctor and the Soul*) when he admonishes us that in cases where a cure is no longer possible, our humanity demands that we offer comfort and solace (1986, pp. 267-284). And Lukas in *Meaning in Suffering* reiterates, "Therapists, who limit themselves to what is curable, practice their profession but fail in their vocation" (1986, p.62). She continues by pointing out that people who have not learned to accept fate, who believe they can get almost everything for a price, are likely to despair when faced with unavoidable suffering. In a crisis only three possibilities are open to them, namely: (1) Faith and a belief in God. (2) Empathy and understanding from people around them. (3) Their own stable meaning fulfillment. Dr. Lukas points out why people turn to professionals for comfort in ever increasing numbers:

> Faith in God has been shaken in many people's lives, and interpersonal support even more so.... People to whom we turn in such a crisis have shifted from minister and family

> to the psychotherapist. In our loneliness we seek from strangers what we can no longer find in a firm faith or from people close to us. Psychotherapists, this "last hope," cannot afford to say, "Here I cannot help; this goes beyond my field of competence." Where scientific knowledge fails, humanity must take over (Lukas, 1986, p. 62).

This is true, even more so, for the caregivers working in pastoral psychology. Compassion is hardly ever listed as a required course in the curriculum of our professional training, yet it may be the only course that requires a passing grade in the curriculum of life. It is our vocation in life, not only as professionals but also as human beings, to help others bear their suffering—physical, psychological, even spiritual—when suffering is unavoidable and fate must be accepted.

How do we comfort? By listening attentively—listening is an act of love that opens the door to the interior of the other. We comfort by being available—being present to another human being who is in pain or anguish is a self-transcending act. It requires courage to offer to help carry another's burden. It is a spiritual gift we bestow when we are there for others in their time of crisis, or time of need, that calls for comforting.

The comforting aspect of logotherapy was termed "medical ministry" by Frankl. This "comforting" through medical ministry is explicated in *Viktor Frankl's Logotherapy: Meaning-Centered Interventions* as follows:

> 1. When cure is no longer possible, *medical ministry* is called for. Medical ministry is that aspect within the logotherapeutic system that deals with situations where the physical cause of the condition cannot be eliminated. Then the atti-

tudinal value related to finding meaning in suffering is an appropriate approach in therapeutic interactions. A recommended method for interaction with a person in this situation is called the "parable method." The therapist tells a story or a parable aimed at making the point that suffering and illness must be accepted as part of the human condition.

2. A second method that Frankl advised involved using the Socratic dialogue (Frankl, 1969, WTM p. 117-141). This method of comforting was demonstrated in *Man's Search for Meaning* as follows:

> Once, an elderly general practitioner consulted me because of his severe depression. He could not overcome the loss of his wife who had died two years before and whom he had loved above all else. Now, how could I help him? What should I tell him? Well, I refrained from telling him anything but instead confronted him with the question, 'What would have happened, Doctor, if you had died first, and your wife would have had to survive you?' 'Oh,' he said, 'for her this would have been terrible; how she would have suffered!' Whereupon I replied, 'You see, Doctor, such a suffering has been spared her, and it was you who have spared her this suffering–to be sure, at the price that now you have to survive and mourn her.' He said no word but shook my hand and calmly left my office. In some way, suffering ceases to be suffering at the moment it finds a meaning, such as the meaning of sacrifice' (Frankl, 1959, p. 135).

3. The third means of therapeutically addressing unavoidable suffering and death involves communicating to the person the belief that the past is a secure storehouse where all of life's accomplishments are accumulated and never lost. Frankl held a firm conviction that it is the responsibility of the physician not only to treat physical illness, but also to comfort the person under the physician's care.

4. Frankl believed religious faith to be a human phenomenon and as such it must be taken seriously from a psychological perspective. Taking a serious approach to religion allows the therapist to utilize the spiritual resources of the person. Spiritual is defined in this instance as being a unique and truly human aspect of human beings, and therefore an authentic area of concern for a therapist (Rice, et al., 2002, Chap. VII).

The caregiver working with pastoral psychology will find many opportunities to *comfort* and, perhaps, to implement some of these approaches logotherapists have found to be helpful.

Existential / Phenomenological Intervention

Since the term *existential* is subject to many interpretations, the definition used in this context indicates *having being within given circumstances*. Existentialism acknowledges that each of us must face important and difficult situations, make decisions with limited knowledge, within a given time frame. Thus, we shape our existence. Clients presenting for pastoral psychotherapy are seeking help with problems in their existence (life), and they need timely help.

Phenomenology denotes how consciousness is expressed in human experience. Frankl defined phenomenology as an attempt to describe the way a person understands self (1969, WTM, p. 7). Phenomenology is concerned not only with *being*, but also with *becoming*. That implies, we challenge clients to grow beyond their current base line of functioning.

When we speak of existential/phenomenological intervention, we mean how one individual human being experiences a given situation. We take that person out of an assigned category and treat him individually. We avoid reductionistic dictates that only address behaviors and psychic drives and we involve his noetic consciousness, as far as possible, in making choices for his life. We seek to expand his awareness of choices available to him at the time. We assist that person to find meaningful goals, which have value for him, that are attainable. We encourage, we support, but we do not coerce. The responsibility for change rests with the client, not the logotherapist.

Existential/phenomenological intervention is focused on the present and is directed to the future, not the past. While the intervention is experiential, the importance of human intuition, as a means to gain knowledge, is accepted. The following incidence in Frankl's own life demonstrates this premise.

In the preface to the third edition of *The Doctor and the Soul* (1986), Viktor Frankl describes how one day (during his concentration camp experience as he limped along painfully in a long column of men in the bitter cold) deploring the misery of his life, he forced his thoughts to turn to another subject. He describes for us what happened:

> Suddenly I saw myself standing on the platform of a well-lit, warm, and pleasant lecture room. In front of me sat an attentive audience on comfortable upholstered seats. I was

> giving a lecture... All that oppressed me at that moment became objective, seen and described from a remote viewpoint of science. By this method I succeeded somehow in rising above the situation, above the sufferings of the moment, and I observed them as if they were already of the past (Frankl, 1986, p. xi)

This passage had intrigued me for years. I wondered, do we have to be in extremis before we can accomplish this shift in awareness to what might be termed "phase transition to non-local time"—experiences occurring outside of our usual time/space continuum? My success with what I have come to call the "logoanchor technique" tells me that we do not. It is a technique for entering another ontological dimension at will, and having experiences similar to the one described above by Frankl—experiences which help us to rise above the suffering of the moment. It is a means to gain strength to carry on in spite of very painful situations or circumstances that are inescapable at the moment.

In a professional field where great value is placed on quantifiable data, existential therapy, particularly with phenomenological aspects, is a homeless waif. Symbolic representations and noetic interventions are difficult to measure because they cannot be randomly duplicated. Each client's experience will be unique. Even when the same technique is used, no two therapeutic experiences or outcomes will be alike because the client's circumstances and the therapist's approach should be individual, not categorical. Nonetheless, these interventions may be the most applicable in dealing with existential dilemmas that are brought before us, and need to be addressed by caregivers practicing pastoral psychology.

When one goes to do battle on these intense fronts of life, it is best to wear the armor of vulnerability and to reach into the noetic or spiritual dimension for strength and invincibility. The noetic dimension is where the essence of humanness can be found. This is the High Country to which logotherapy as a *Höhenpsychologie* (height-psychology) leads the way.

Improvisation, creativity, imagination and, above all, individuation, are required to reach therapeutic goals when working with existential/phenomenological interventions. Frankl was fond of saying, "If I treat two of my patient's alike, I have mistreated at least one of them."

The Logoanchor Technique

The logoanchor technique was inspired by Viktor Frankl's experience of shifting his focus in an intolerable situation to a desirable possibility, as previously described. This can occur spontaneously, as was the case with Frankl. It can be argued that it was, clinically speaking, a hallucination. (In his experience, if we want to call it a "hallucination," may have been brought on or exacerbated by starvation and fatigue.) However, the strength he derived from this experience helped him to survive against great odds—not only physically, but psycho-spiritually by giving him hope. The hope that some day he might be able to give a lecture on his life work sustained him. He had a "*Why*" to live for—a meaning to fulfill.

One can learn to enter a state of expanded awareness at will (with some practice) where one can access the noetic unconscious more readily. Formerly unthought of possibilities, in answer to urgent life questions, often present themselves in that state, which surprise client and therapist alike.

In a difficult counseling situation once, when I reached the point of desperation, thinking, "The textbooks did not prepare me for this!" I began to improvise. As a result, the *logoanchor technique* was born. Now I often employ what I think of as the logoanchor: An experience, rich in meaning, either from the past, or an anticipated one from the future (a là Frankl), which can be used as an anchor in a currently troubling situation. This technique can be used effectively in many situations. For example, to comfort frightened children, to help the lonely feel less isolated, to bridge communication gaps between partners, to deal with inerasable guilt, to help heal grief and loss, to face the fear of dying, and to find motivation for living.

The **logoanchor technique** guides clients in the search for anchoring experiences in their own lives. Anchoring experiences are times when individuals were in touch with the highest or noblest they are capable of, such as: moments in life that were deeply meaningful, times of intuitive knowing, bursts of insight; also, experiences of altruistic love, boundless gratitude, heightened creativity, faith, hope, sacred and authentic moments. These are the precious moments to relive and savor. Most likely these were the times when the noetic energies flowed abundantly. The intention of this method is to get the client back into the flow of noetic energy, to reconnect with that vital life force again, through the activation of a **logoanchor**.

The *logoanchor technique* is not something I would use with a new client; not until I discerned a readiness to introduce it. Some may not reach the stage where they ever want to try it, because there are elements of relinquishing conscious control associated with it. As a closed eye process, the logoanchor technique takes us beyond waking consciousness to an area closer to the noetic region. A preparatory explanation of the technique needs to be given so the client can decide if the closed eye process appeals to him. Where that is not the case, we search for logoanchors by recalling times of greater attunement to one's core or center from memory.

It is optimal to begin the multi-sensory process with a brief relaxation. Many clients already have a means to do that. For those who don't, I use the following simple method. Speaking slowly, I will say something along these lines:

I would like to invite you to participate in a multi-sensory imagery process. Let's begin by closing your eyes or by focusing on one point to avoid visual distraction. Get comfortable in your seat, feeling that your body is well supported and safe.

When you have done that, take a deep breath, and as you exhale let go of any physical tensions... just relax.

Take another deep breath, and let go of any emotional tensions you may have while you exhale... just let them go.

Take one more deep breath, and when you exhale let go of your mental preoccupations... just let them drift away... and be here now... totally present to yourself in this moment in time.

Begin breathing in your own natural rhythm now... a rhythm uniquely yours... breathing that will help you stay calm and centered.

Now let your consciousness drift, the way you do when you daydream. Let us go down memory lane in search of an experience that filled you with awe and wonder; to a time when you felt most integrated and vitally alive! Look for a time when you were in touch with your uniqueness, your humanness in an essential way.

Was there a time in your life when you felt expansive... full of intuitive knowing... or experienced something sacred? Was there an instant when you felt transcendence was not only possible, but immanent? Perhaps a moment when you loved the whole world and everyone in it?

Bring that state of awareness forward to the present moment and cherish it.

Imprint the experience in your conscious memory now through multi-sensory impressions:

See the memory clearly before you.

Hear the sounds that accompanied the experience again.

What tastes were involved? Was it sweet, sour, bitter, salty, spicy?

Notice the smells, odors, aromas or fragrances that accompanied the experience.

What was it like to the touch? What emotions were evoked?

Put as many of these sensory impressions as you can together now into a holographic image and fully re-experience that moment again that was very life-giving... knowing that it is still alive within you and that you can use it again and again as a logoanchor whenever you are in need of one.

Give the client enough time to savor the experience, then ask him to return to the "here and now" by slowly opening his eyes and orienting himself to the external environment. The inner experience the client has just had needs to be remembered and brought to conscious awareness. This can be done through sharing it with the therapist, writing it down, drawing or painting it, etc. Again, the more senses that can be involved in the externalization of the experience, the better future recall of the logoanchor will be. An example of the usefulness of the logoanchor technique follows.

Application of the Logoanchor Technique:

Lisa, a young woman with whom I was working in therapy, had suffered grievous losses in the preceding two years. First, her mother died of cancer. It had been difficult for Lisa to watch her mother deteriorate as the illness progressed.

The family had barely adjusted to mother's death, when her father died suddenly of a heart attack. Lisa had been very close to her father. "I felt heart-broken when my dad died," said Lisa, "and I became very ill with bacterial endocarditis." [Inflammation of the lining of the heart] *Weak from the prolonged illness and unable to function, she lost her job. Instead of doing familiar work competently, she suddenly found herself having to deal with probate matters and other totally bewildering things concerning her parents' legal affairs.*

Then her brother, John, whom she loved dearly, came to ask her if he could move in with her. He was dying and wanted to be near her. She nursed John at home between hospitalizations for several months, until he died of lung cancer. Lisa haltingly explained, "John was my best friend since childhood. Suddenly I have no family... I am so alone... I'm afraid to be alone... I can't sleep... I miss them so much... I feel so forsaken... there is no one who loves me now." Lisa was truly overwhelmed by grief and loss.

Gradually I began a Socratic dialogue by probing, "Lisa, let us look for a time in your life when you felt loved, protected, and cared for–not necessarily by your immediate family. Was there ever such a time?"

Lisa: "Yes... when I was a little girl growing up... Our neighbors were Catholic and they had built a little shrine in their backyard. I was always welcome there. Often I would pick flowers and put them on the little altar, then I would sit there for hours and talk to God and the Blessed Mother. I really thought that God lived in that little shrine! I always felt so at home there–very safe, protected, and loved!"

She had found a logoanchor! Dereflection from her present grief and fear of being alone had begun through a shift in focus to an experience that had been supportive in her past. We tapped into that memory and made it more vivid and accessible through multi-sensory imagery. She was to entertain that memory whenever she felt forsaken or when she couldn't sleep. She could readily do this alone after the initial process in the office.

After practicing the logoanchor technique daily for two weeks (of being in that little shrine where she felt safe and loved by God and the Blessed Mother), on a subsequent visit she happily told me, "We seem to have our family reunions there now! First, John joined me one day in that little shrine in my mind. It was such fun; I could make him any age I wanted him to be. Then my dad showed up. I was very comforted by his presence. Now mom joins us. She looks beautiful again. It's great! I feel so much better and I can sleep!"

Post-Notes: In the physical dimension Lisa could not change her situation, nor bring back to life those she loves. In the psychological dimension she was overwhelmed by her losses to the point where she could not function. Only in the noetic dimension was she free to take a stand against her suffering. She chose to transform her grief into gratitude for all the love she had known in her family; and, for everything that had been beautiful in her past, which helped her to transcend her tragedy. She discovered rich meanings in her past and used them as building blocks for her future.

Pastoral caregivers surely must first be comfortable with core issues of human existence, such as *life, death, love,* and the *sufferings* that arise from them, in order to be empathic listeners and serve as guides to others, who are trying to transcend their existential crises. Pastoral caregivers, to be effective, will need to have compassion, experiential maturity, and spiritual poise. They will also need to be firmly centered in their noetic core when entreated daily to serve those who may have lost touch with their core.

Pastoral Trauma Intervention

When a trauma has occurred that taxes the coping skills of an individual beyond the point where adaptive living is possible, the need for effective intervention is clearly indicated. Timely, skillful and sensitive intervention may greatly reduce the need for long-term care.

Since psycho-spiritual wounds are less easily seen than physical wounds, it is well to be reminded that people can "bleed to death" from them nonetheless. These invisible wounds will need to be treated psychotherapeutically, just as physical wounds would need to be treated medically. In order to restore the person having suffered trauma to vigorous mental health, compassionate support is necessary. Then, hopefully, a person having suffered psycho-spiritual wounds can even transcend his former baseline level of functioning, due to the growth that has resulted from surviving the trauma. The following example will illustrate that premise:

A *Case Study on Trauma Intervention* (LK)

I received a telephone call one day from a young husband (a member of our church), who seemed to be at the end of his endurance. He explained that he was greatly concerned about the mental state of his pregnant wife. She had suddenly become unable to cope with things and he was desperately seeking help. Shortly thereafter, the young couple appeared at the church counseling office and I learned about the horrendous trauma his wife had undergone recently.

About three weeks prior she had received a call from the sheriff's office of her home town asking her to come to the morgue to identify a body - feared to be the mutilated remains of her twin sister, who had not been in touch with family for some time ("Since she began running around with a 'wild crowd,'" according to her family.) With great trepidation LK went to the sheriff's office hoping that her worst fears regarding her sister would be dispelled.

She explained, "They really tried to prepare me for what I would see, but nothing could have prepared me for THAT sight! My dear, beautiful sister... It was my sister. I could make positive identification that it was she... Now I can't get the image of her mutilated, decomposing body out of my mind. That horrible sight is always before my eyes. It haunts me day and night."

And LK continued, "I'm terrified of the dark now because IT stares at me. I'm afraid to close my eyes because she's there. I can't sleep because of the nightmares I have. I hold on to my husband and beg him not to go to work and leave me alone at home. I panic when I'm left alone with IT. My in-laws have been very sympathetic and good to me, but everyone is getting tired of my 'state.' What am I going to do? How will I take care of my baby when it's born? Am I crazy..?"

Here was an existential crisis brought on by severe trauma that called for intervention on every level of being: physical, psychological and spiritual. As her therapist I had the "home turf" advantage. This young woman felt safe in the church and she trusted me. While being totally present to her through active listening, I sensed her deep anguish and distress.

I encouraged her to let the tears flow, to let the anger out, to talk about her fears. The afternoon passed as she agonized over what she had seen and railed against God for allowing such a fate to befall her sister. She feared that she would never get rid of that horrible sight embedded in her mind.

As evening fell, she was exhausted. A catharsis had taken place, an emptying out. It was time to begin reconstruction. We began with a relaxation technique that brought her close to the threshold between the waking and sleep state (a drowsy state of awareness that is optimal for transforming inner images and symbols). I asked LK to go down memory lane, back to her childhood, and look for scenes with her sister (the twins had been very close in childhood, but drifted apart as young adults). She sleepily described some of the scenes from her memory; and, I suggested she select her favorite image of her sister, to let it permeate her mind, and to hold it and cherish it. [The Logoanchor technique was used].

In the meantime, it had grown dark outside. I had not turned on the light in the counseling room. We sat in the dark as she continued to talk about her childhood with her sister, how close they were, and how beautiful it was then. I left the room on a pretext without turning on the light, and observed her from a distance. She did not exhibit signs of panic when left alone in the dark. She was tired and sad, but composed. I felt, she was ready to go home. The therapist's prescription to LK was: "Entertain these images from your memory of good times with your sister; eat a good meal; take a relaxing bath and go to sleep!" She was to call me the next day.

The following day, LK reported having slept well and long. When frightening images intruded themselves, she was able to superimpose happier ones and the intruders faded away. She felt she was regaining control over her thoughts again. With the most debilitating symptoms reduced, therapy could be focused on other trauma related issues.

It was foreseeable that pain over the loss of her sibling would set in as the shock of the trauma wore off. Intense feelings of grief soon surfaced. The death of her only sister, her twin, was very painful. During this phase her faith was an invaluable resource. Belief in an afterlife was a great comfort to her.

Grieving took time. Eventually she was able to transcend her loss by extending herself beyond her own grief and reach out to others; and, she looked forward to the new baby that would soon join their lives. Her newly found strength became evident when she took the initiative to help her parents face the loss of their child. Through her mediation, they were able to deal with their grief better. She reminded them that the love they had bestowed upon their children was not lost, but lives on. This is obvious, she told them, visible in the depth of their grief, which is also an expression of their love. If they had not cared so deeply for their children, their loss would not be so devastating now. Strength she did not know she had was emerging. LK had not only survived the trauma, she had also matured in many ways.

Post-Notes: In the preceding case, my concern during therapy had been that post traumatic stress syndrome may develop, where involuntary intrusive images would haunt LK for the rest of her life. Follow-up care consisted of reinforcing the healthy and happy images she carried in her memory of her sister. Reminding her that she was in charge of her inner life, helped to strengthen her will. Choosing the images she wanted to entertain—with their accompanying feelings—was something she practiced during after-care. This helped to restore her sense of being in charge of her inner world and no longer the victim of intrusive images that had so distressed her and rendered her helpless.

During a recent telephone follow-up call, I learned that the little family of three was well and thriving. Let me give credit where credit is due: This case was under the aegis of Grace! It is well to invoke divine assistance when working in pastoral care and to give thanks humbly when it is bestowed.

A Word about After-Care

Assuming appropriate trauma intervention took place during the acute phase of a given crisis, and the person is able to resume handling life situations in an accustomed way, then the time of discharge from therapy is approaching. How this last treatment phase is handled may make a tremendous difference whether the person returns to former levels of coping or emerges with net gains of inner strength due to the traumatic experience undergone.

One way of encouraging post-traumatic growth is through supportive after-care. Follow-up care is seen in some quarters as a luxury item in intervention. Yet the importance of after-care cannot be underestimated in preventing relapse from occurring.

I have yet to experience anything but appreciation for a sincerely extended personal inquiry about a client's progress. At the very least, it is a professional courtesy extended; at best, a brief authentic encounter concerning someone's well-being, who has entrusted details of his life to the therapist that few have been privileged to.

Occasionally, this outreach has served as recognition by the client that further work would be helpful.

Follow-up calls by telephone have been found to be far preferable to letters or forms to be filled out and returned. It is the human element that counts. Especially in the aftermath of a traumatic experience, clients need to know that someone cares about their well-being. The follow-up call can also serve to keep the door open for future interventions, if needed. It is preferable by far to do a little preventive work in potentially problematic situations, lest they become full blown crises requiring trauma intervention.

Vital Elements in Logotherapeutic Treatment Planning

As we have seen in the foregoing examples logotherapeutic treatment planning begins with meeting the client where he is. The therapist must be willing to enter the client's existential paradigm. This will often lead to a catharsis whereby pent-up anguish is released. The client having unburdened himself will feel better for the time being. The short-term goal has been accomplished–he feels better! This is well as a first step, and can serve as a way to build a trust bridge between the client and the therapist. However, it is dangerous to quit there, or to allow the client to use the therapist only for cathartic outbursts in the future. To achieve long-term goals, commitment to do what is necessary to effect transformation in the client's life is needed. As demonstrated in the case studies given in the last two chapters, a therapeutic progression can be noted. Often beginning with catharsis, the process will lead through:

1. Distancing from Symptoms
2. Modification of Attitudes
3. Reduction of Symptoms
4. Orientation toward Meaningful Goals.

1. Distancing from Symptoms:

   The first task is to help clients realize that they are not their symptoms. They are helped to see that fears, obsessions, depressions, feelings of inferiority, and emotional outbreaks are not who they are but simply qualities they have that can be modified and, perhaps, overcome. Clients learn that they can change unwanted habits and patterns. In cases of unavoidable suffering (death, loss) it is possible to change one's attitude toward blows of fate.

   Self-distancing is utilized to get clients to view themselves from the outside; to become observers of themselves and their situation or circumstance. Methods developed by Frankl and others to accomplish self-distancing are:

   Paradoxical Intention (utilizing humor)
   Dereflection (altered focus)
   Socratic Dialogue (evoking new insights)
   Appealing Technique (suggestions)

   In any event, the therapist cannot rely on persuasion.

2. Modification of Attitudes:

   The importance of our attitudes toward ourselves, our lives and our difficulties has been a crucial discovery of psychotherapy. It is important to assess attitudes, especially of clients in that gray area between psychological illness and mental health. It's usually not the problem or difficulty the person is experiencing that causes the distress, but the attitude the person has toward it. An unhealthy attitude can block inner forces, which could overcome suffering and distress, and pushes the individual into a passive role in which one feels like a helpless victims of circumstances. An unhealthy attitude is always in some way linked with passivity, negation, resignation, often with despair, stagnation and indifference.

When the defiant power of the human spirit is activated, a shift occurs or a modification of attitude results. This promotes the "will to meaning" and modulates attitudes toward the positive. Healthy attitudes offer strong protection against psychological illness and foster a high ability to bear suffering in crisis situations. A positive attitude is one that brings harmony with one's own conscience, teaches courage and dignity, and promotes growth through changing the self.

In severe illness, paralysis, amputations, loss of significant loved one by death, the attitude determines how the unavoidable is accepted. One does not have to be defeated by suffering. The defiant power of the spirit enables the individual to turn unavoidable suffering into a human achievement, even a human triumph. Logotherapy here deals with the nous (spirit). The therapist needs to assist the client to move from the egocentric world-view—through self-transcendence—beyond the victim stance, to a health-giving attitude and existence.

3. Reduction of Symptoms:

   Following successful modification of attitudes symptoms usually become manageable or disappear. When a symptom is caused by circumstances beyond control (i.e., loss of a loved one, physical decrease), a healthy attitude helps persons accept their fate so they can bear the pain without succumbing to despair. The Socratic Dialogue can be employed in drawing attention to the achievement of having conquered their symptoms, or to the heroic stance taken toward an unchangeable fate.

4. Orientation toward Meaningful Goals:

As symptoms are reduced, disappear or become bearable, the client can be oriented toward meaningful activities and experiences. Logotherapy is ultimately very pragmatic. Existential analysis may give us insights into the problem or situation at hand, but we need to move into commitment to something or someone. Direction needs to be found that will lead to a more fulfilling and meaning-centered future.

The uniqueness of the individual must be considered. Activities and experiences will only be healing if they are self-chosen. Orientation toward values that can be found in experiences, activities or attitudes will have to reflect the innate talents and qualities of the client–giving them authentic expression will be healing. (The foregoing segment on logotherapeutic treatment planning was compiled from works by Lukas, Fabry, and Welter; it was first presented by Graber and Rogina, 2001, in the course, *Logotherapeutic Model of Mental Health*, Chap. VIII.)

When the above process or therapeutic flow is followed, it leads to psychotherapeutic success that is most likely to survive long-term. Logotherapy is not a "quick-fix" nor is it long-drawn analysis. It does require substantial functioning of the higher processes of conscious experience or cognition. Organically damaged or severely disturbed clients may not be able to function at this level; although, many of these may be helped by logotherapeutic interventions when cognition clears (i.e., in substance abuse after detoxification or after the acute phase of mental illness has been medically addressed).

As mentioned previously, after-care or postvention will often serve as sensible prevention, especially by providing comfort where cure is no longer possible. Compassionate concern exhibited by the caregiver is like a healing balm. Dr. Lukas' admonition, "Where scientific knowledge fails, humanity must take over" best summarizes the attitude the caregiver is called upon to bring to this vocation and helping profession.

Pitfalls to Avoid

If the warning, "Don't play psychiatrist!" directed at therapists who are not medically trained or duly licensed to perform psychiatric services is valid, perhaps the warning to pastoral psychologists should be, "Don't play God!" The pastoral counselor runs a particular risk of causing iatrogenic or helper induced damage because people who seek our services often ascribe a spiritual status to us that is usually unfounded. They readily place their trust in us and are cruelly disappointed when it is betrayed. The disappointment may not be due to real or intended harm, but to clients' unrealistic expectations of what a pastoral psychologist (in the role of minister, priest, rabbi, counselor, or pastoral caregiver) has to offer. Frankl was well aware of this danger and even found a term for it, "ecclesiogenic neurosis" (*Will to Meaning*, 1988, p. 132) or clergy induced damage.

Aside from downright abuse, *ecclesiogenic* damage can result inadvertently when a client's guilt or fears are exacerbated, particularly when this leads to a loss of hope. Many a good "Hellfire and Brimstone" sermon has done exactly that. Since clergy is often seen as being "the voice for God," whatever is said by a member of the clergy—even in a counseling situation—tends to carry greater moral weight than would be the case with a secular counselor.

Conversely, this very "prestige suggestion" can have a beneficent influence on those who seek the services of pastoral counselors. Since clients tend to give our counsel more credence, interventions facilitated by pastoral psychologists can be deeply meaningful and healing precisely because they are taken to heart.

IX

RELEVANT INCLUSIONS and COMPARISONS

American Schools of Psychology

On the American scene we witness a different course of development in psychological theories than the progression observed in the Viennese schools of psychotherapy. There, each new wave of thought or school was an outgrowth of its antecedent: Adlerian *Individual Psychology* grew out of and developed beside Freudian *Psychoanalysis*. Frankl's *Existential Analysis* and *Logotherapy*, in turn, built on the existing framework and grew beyond it. There was overlapping that provided continuity, yet stimulated growth and expansion of theories, and devised treatment methods that went beyond what the preceding wave had offered (depicted in Fig. 1).

The Psychoanalytic Movement in the United States

After psychotherapy had established itself enough to be taken seriously as a science and a distinct field of study, the first European wave or movement to reach the American shores was *Psychoanalysis*. Brought over by students and disciples of Freud, it spread quickly during the 1920s and became later known in the United States as the *First Force* in psychology. Being a lengthy psychoanalytic process it was a therapist-dominated and dependent approach by its very nature.

The classical model of psychoanalysis (as taught by Freud) has undergone changes and considerable development since it crossed the Atlantic. A first adaptation introduced was the *Interpersonal Model* (in the 1930s and 1940s), whereby the client/therapist were seen as participant/observer. In this adaptation the psychoanalytic process became more co-creative and less therapist dominated. Also, the focus included the "here and now" and was no longer solely retrospective.

Later (1950s), an import from England, the *Object Relations Theory*, impacted the psychoanalytic movement. This theory postulates that relationships (beginning with the mother-infant dyad and early group experiences) are decisive influences in forming intrapsychic images in the infant and growing child for developing its identity. And, that these internal constructs become the basis of mental organization in subsequent interactions with others in friendship, marriage, and rearing of family.

A further influence (1970s) came from the *Deconstruction Movement* in philosophy. Its inclusion of epistemology and phenomenology acknowledged subjective aspects of clients' experiences and moved beyond the purely objective observer role of the therapist.

The latest American-bred variation is the *Relational Model* of psychoanalysis. Since its beginning in the 1980s, this innovation has gained in popularity. It combines aspects of the interpersonal model and the object/relations model. In the US the movement is centered in New York, but has a strong following (with local flavor) beyond the US, particularly in South America.

Most contemporary schools of psychoanalysis no longer subscribe to Freud's premise that all unconscious conflict is rooted in frustrated sexual and aggressive drives, but hold a broader view. In spite of the innovations that have occurred since the traditional Freudian approach, psychoanalysis has retained its identity as a distinct treatment methodology and has not been absorbed into subsequent systems. The analysand (client) is in psychoanalysis typically for several years, and the role of the analyst (therapist) is still very prominent.

Behavior Therapy and Behaviorism

Behaviorism had its inception in North America as early as 1913, and was later joined by many other influences, including developments in psychology from Russia and England. According to behaviorism, virtually all behavior can be explained as a product of learning or conditioning. Its theoretical goal was to predict and control behavior. The distinctive feature of the behavioral approach is its emphasis on modifying specific observable behaviors (using principles of learning theory) and to modify or change self-defeating behaviors or habits.

Although it ignited the imagination of many experimenters and researchers early on, its wide-spread dissemination occurred after WW-II with the further inclusion of *Cognitive Therapy* into the cause and effect equation of behavior. The cognitive approach reintroduces mental content into behavior modification. Emotional problems are attributed to cognitive errors that produce negative patterns (distorted and self-defeating thoughts). The implication in treatment is that by changing clients' thoughts, the feelings around them and, consequently, the behavior they result in will change as well. To that end many methods were developed (Hypnotherapy, Sex Therapy, Rational-Emotive Therapy, Reality Therapy, Brief Therapy, and others). Cognitive therapy, often combined with behavior therapy, is referred to as "cognitive-behavioral" therapy and is the most widely used approach in the US currently. It places emphasis on curing symptoms in the present, rather than looking for causes in the past. *Behavior Therapy* or *Behaviorism* became known as the *Second Force* in American psychology.

Humanistic-Existential Psychology

Psychoanalysis and Behaviorism tended to be antagonistic toward each other. Their proponents failed to see that each looked at different aspects of the human phenomenon. Another major wave arose in the 1960s and became known as *Humanistic-Existential Psychology*. It saw more of the whole person and attempted to unify the prevailing fragmentation in the field of psychology and its approaches to treatment. Unable to bridge the gulf between Psychoanalysis and Behaviorism, it too became a separate movement in psychology. While the archaic point of view limited psychology to the sensory aspects of experience, existential psychology is concerned with observing and understanding inner experiences of a person. It emphasized the capacity to live fully in the present and to respond freely and flexibly to new experiences without Angst (fear).

In existential analysis clients or analysands explore their own being: their values, relationships, and commitments. The objective of therapy is not to learn to acquire better coping skills, but to develop more fulfilling modes of existence. The emphasis is on "becoming" rather than on static and fixed being. Humanistic-existential psychotherapy addresses more of the entire person instead of just one aspect, such as unconscious drives or behaviors. It deals with subjective experiences, freedom of choice, and realization of potential.

The approach to therapy is more interactive, even client-centered. Largely psychodynamic, it includes numerous well-established and some explorative therapies (Jungian analysis, Rogerian client-centered method, Gestalt Therapy, Transactional Analysis, and others). Humanistic-Existential Psychology is considered the *Third Force* among American schools of psychology. It is future-oriented and places responsibility for change on the client, not the therapist.

Transpersonal Psychology

Since the late 1960s a new branch, *Transpersonal Psychology*, has been emerging and was definitely on the scene by the 1980s. It may have a short history, but it has a long past. Many of its adherents see it as a blending of ancient wisdom and modern science or between Eastern mysticism and Western rationalism. The movement was spawned by the disaffections of those who felt that psychology (neither Psychoanalysis, Behaviorism, nor Humanistic-Existential psychology) adequately addressed states of consciousness that were being experienced by some, which seemed to point at exceptional levels of psycho-spiritual health, not pathology (as had been described by William James in *The Varieties of Religious Experience*, for instance).

"Transpersonal" literally means "beyond" or "across" the personal psyche. It refers to the extension of consciousness beyond ego boundaries. It is concerned with: values, the sacred in life, the meaning of life and death, unitive consciousness, cosmic awareness, compassion and transpersonal cooperation; and, a number of states of consciousness and experiences that are difficult to describe in linear language (phenomena that are subjective and ephemeral are often termed "mystical", which is a nebulous definition). Some equate "transpersonal" with spiritual and insist that these states of awareness need to be studied along with the conventionally accepted states of being.

As an interdisciplinary and cross-cultural movement, the transpersonal orientation looks to many sources, besides empirical research, for inspiration and validation: References to expanded states of awareness can be found in the esoteric traditions of East and West: Zen Buddhism, Yoga, Sufism, Christian mystical literature, altered states of consciousness research, and others. The transpersonal model is not intended to invalidate the earlier mod-

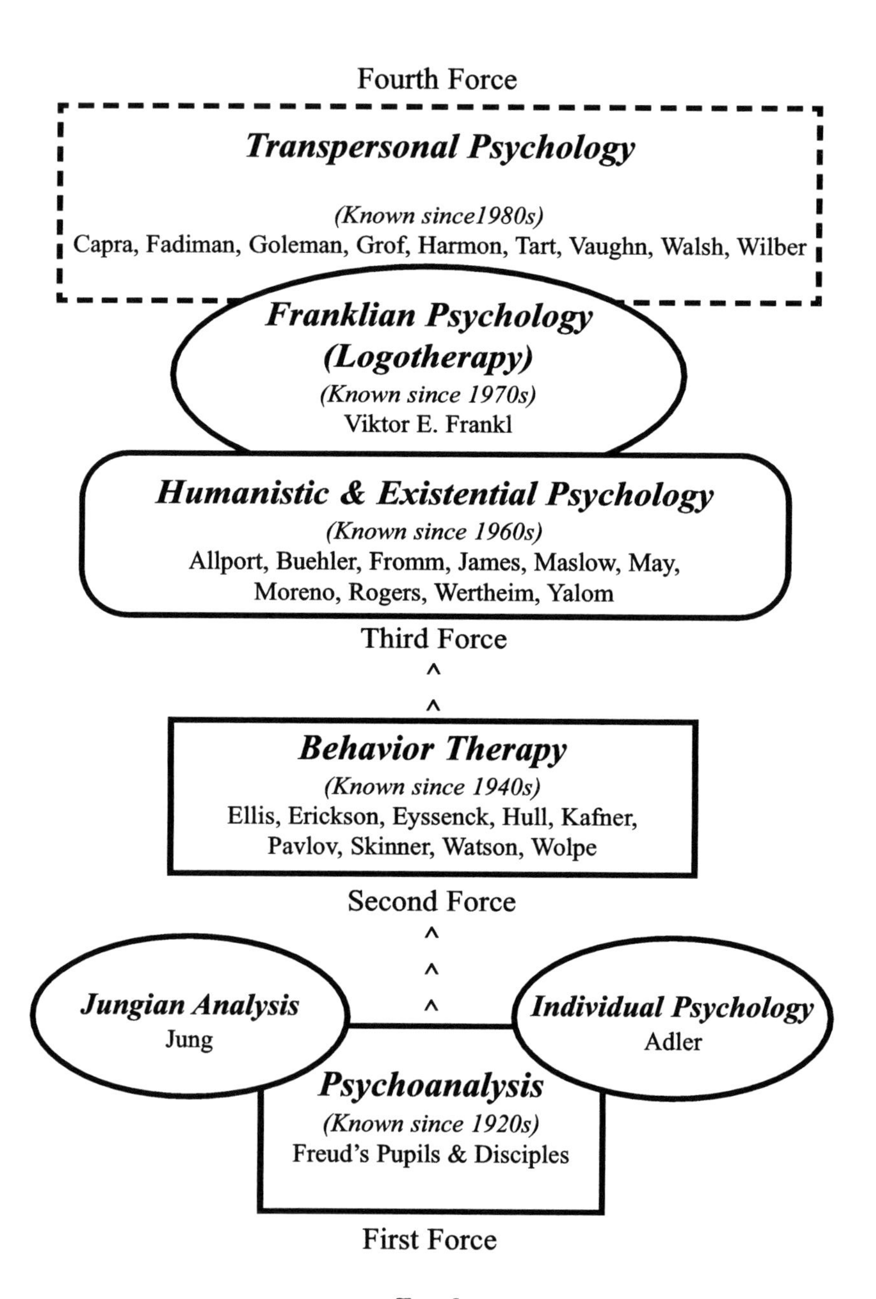
AMERICAN SCHOOLS OF PSYCHOTHERAPY
Fourth Force
Transpersonal Psychology
(Known since1980s)
Capra, Fadiman, Goleman, Grof, Harmon, Tart, Vaughn, Walsh, Wilber
Franklian Psychology
(Logotherapy)
(Known since 1970s)
Viktor E. Frankl
Humanistic & Existential Psychology
(Known since 1960s)
Allport, Buehler, Fromm, James, Maslow, May,
Moreno, Rogers, Wertheim, Yalom
Third Force
Behavior Therapy
(Known since 1940s)
Ellis, Erickson, Eyssenck, Hull, Kafner,
Pavlov, Skinner, Watson, Wolpe
Second Force
Jungian Analysis
Jung
Individual Psychology
Adler
Psychoanalysis
(Known since 1920s)
Freud's Pupils & Disciples
First Force

Fig. 8

els of psychology, but to expand our concepts of human nature and our place in the universal scheme of things. Transpersonal Psychology (with the inclusion of the human spirit in its ontology) sees self-transcendence as the pinnacle of human growth. Still a developing field, this *Fourth Force* appears to be inclusive of many streams of wisdom and holds promise for the future. In the US, Transpersonal Psychology appears to be primarily a West Coast phenomenon at this stage.

Franklian Psychology among Other Schools of Thought

In the preceding chart (Fig. 8) Franklian psycholgy having ideological elements of both, *Humanistic / Existential Psychology* and *Transpersonal Psychology*, was positioned as an ideal bridge between the *Third* and *Fourth Force* in psychology. Frankl's existential analysis is rooted in existential psychology and has a *third force* posture, yet his logotherapy advocates self-transcendence and recognizes the human spirit as the source of strengths in the manner of the *fourth force* movement.

Please note: Adlerian individual psychology and Jungian analysis (being psychoanalytic in origin) were shown as outgrowths of that genre (in Fig. 8) even though they went beyond it—each in its own way.

Other Noteworthy Comparisons

There are other ideological bridges that span the field and appear on the horizon out of their time sequence. The most notable among them is William James and his *Pragmatism Theory*.

William James (1842-1910)

It is not possible to talk about the forces in psychology—particularly within the American Schools of Psychology—without mentioning William James who may be considered the "Søren Kierkegaard" of America. It was James' *Pragmatism Theory* that established the practical and empirical participation of the "human factor" in psychology and philosophy. James' ideas have also influenced his contemporary, Edmund Husserl, philosopher and founder of *phenomenology*. Husserl in turn influenced Max Scheler, who had a strong influence on Viktor Frankl.

James' psychology considers many human dimensions: the body, mind, the social and the spiritual dimension. As such, it is a psychology of the self and complements empiricism with the demonstration that human experience plays an essential role in psychotherapy; even a greater role than rational techniques and theories. Even though William James was born more than sixty years before Viktor Frankl, his humanistic and existential ideas embody many similarities to *Logotherapy*. James' *Pragmatism Theory* is empirical, realistic, phenomenological, open and non-reductive. It maintains a value orientation; asks for choices in the human experience; is oriented to the future, while not neglecting past influences on the self; it considers the human spirit as the main defiant power of man. Clearly James' ideas, formulated in the early years of the Twentieth Century, in many ways foreshadowed trends in the social sciences that were to come much later in time (Rice et al., 2002, Chap. III).

Of particular interest to pastoral psychologists would be the reading of William James' *Varieties of Religious Experience*. In this American classic, James approaches the study of religious phenomena in a new way—as a pragmatist *and* as an experimental psychologist. He offers examples of religious thought and life from the widest variety of theological and religious viewpoints.

ଓ

Another psychiatrist whose approach has great appeal to pastoral psychologists, as well as many others, is Carl Jung. A native of Switzerland, America adopted him gladly and his work found wide acceptance. His popularity is still strongly in evidence in spite of the lengthy therapeutic process of Jungian analysis. He, like Frankl, saw the therapeutic possibilities of the human spirit—that is their strong theoretic link.

Carl Gustav Jung (1875-1961)

Carl Jung studied man for over 50 years and amplified our understanding of the subconscious. Jung interpreted mental and emotional disturbances as an attempt to find personal and spiritual wholeness. His work on *word association*, in which a patient's responses to stimulus words revealed what Jung called complexes, brought him international renown and led him to a close collaboration with Austrian psychoanalyst Sigmund Freud. However, Jung declared his independence from Freud's narrow sexual interpretation of the libido by showing the close parallels between ancient myths and psychotic fantasies and by explaining human motivation in terms of a larger creative energy. Although close by geographic proximity and psychoanalytic orientation, Jung is not in direct line of the "Viennese Schools of Psychotherapy."

Especially influential in Jung's theories were the dreams and fantasies of childhood. In *Psychological Types* (1921), he proposed the now well-known personality types, *extrovert* and *introvert*. He later made a distinction between the *personal unconscious*, the repressed feelings and thoughts developed during an individual's life, and the *collective unconscious*, those inherited feelings, thoughts, and memories shared by all humanity. The collective unconscious, according to Jung, is made up of what he called archetypes, or primordial images, that manifest themselves symbolically in religions, myths, fairy tales, and fantasies (*Encarta Encyclopedia*, 2000).

"Meaning" for Frankl and Jung

Both Frankl and Jung saw a close connection between meaning and healing and held that the discovery of meaning in life is essential for psychological health. Jung saw the relationship between neurosis and the lack of meaning when he made the following statement in *Modern Man in Search of a Soul*: "A psychoneurosis must be understood as the suffering of a human being who has not discovered what life means for him" (Jung, 1933, p. 255).

Similarly, Frankl has called the "existential vacuum" or inner emptiness and feeling of meaninglessness, which is experienced by so many, "the collective neurosis of our time" (Frankl, WM, 1988, p. 94). Psychospiritual health can be restored through the pursuit of meaning. The definition of logotherapy, and the motto of the Viktor Frankl Institute of Logotherapy, is: "*Health as Search for Meaning.*"

In an article titled, "Frankl and Jung on Meaning" (IFL, 1992), Thomas Peterson draws attention to the fact that both Frankl and Jung see a close parallel between a person's belief system and psychological health. Frankl was fond of quoting Nietzsche's aphorism: "He who has a why for living, will surmount almost every how." (Frankl, 1967, p. 103). Jung expressed a similar thought when he said: "Man can stand the most incredible hardships when he is convinced that they make sense." (Jung, 1964, p. 76).

Peterson postulates that given the agreement on the role of meaning, one might expect a good deal of similarity between Jung and Frankl on the nature of personality, the conduct of therapy, or the role of the therapist. This is not the case. Peterson's article suggests a possible reason for the disagreement. It first summarizes the respective views on the preferred method of attaining meaning; and, then tries for a "reconciliation strategy" via Jung's theory of types. It is proposed that Frankl is an *extrovert* with an extroverted view of meaning, and Jung is an *introvert* who has provided a complementary interior reading of meaning.

Both strive for anchored commitment. The way they go about it differs. Peterson offers a "Meaning Orientation Model" (Fig. 9) that depicts the strengths and weaknesses of *introversion* and *extroversion*. He states that the introvert will notice and emphasize different aspects of a meaning Gestalt than the extrovert. Each type, giving true testimony of its own perception, will have two different stories to tell. The reconciliation strategy is to accept the testimony of both Frankl and Jung as valid for his own psychological type, thereby obviating fruitless dichotomies. Acceptance of duality of truth then leads to greater understanding and tolerance and is more likely to bring about what both therapeutic approaches hope to accomplish, namely *meaningful living* (Peterson, IFL, 1992, pp. 28-33).

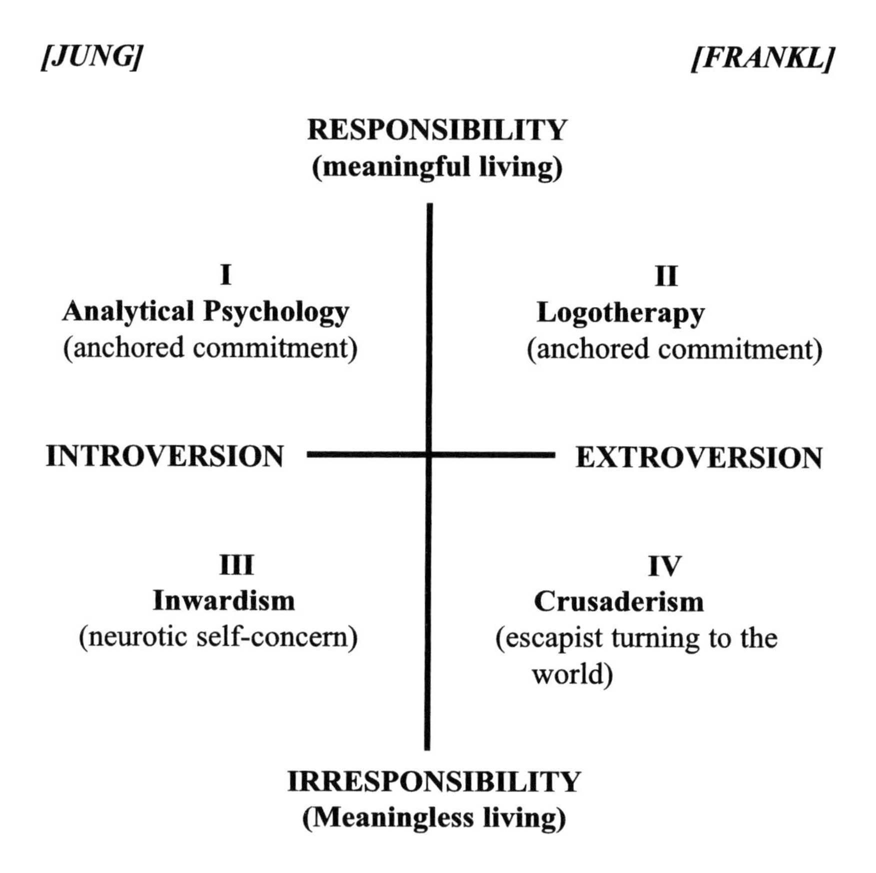

Fig. 9

The above figure presents Peterson's model of four different meaning orientations. The two axes are Responsibility/Irresponsibility and Introversion/Extroversion (psychological type). By crossing the two axes, four possible meaning orientations result.

Peterson explains his **Meaning Orientation Model** as follows:

> **Quadrant I** is Jung's analytical psychology, emphasizing an inner anchoring while at the same time incorporating responsible commitment to the world.
>
> **Quadrant II** is Frankl's logotherapy. It is also an anchored commitment, but with the emphasis on the carrying out the insights gained responsibly and pragmatically..
>
> **Quadrant III** is labeled Inwardism–the neurotic preoccupation with the self. An unbalanced or irresponsible centering on the self prevents the person from taking the necessary actions in the world. Thoughts or ideas without action are empty.
>
> **Quadrant IV** is what Maddi has called "crusaderism." Crusaderism is the throwing of oneself into causes in order to avoid meaninglessness; the meaning of the cause is less important than the fleeting chance to merge oneself into the warmth of the group.

"Avoiding neurotic self-concern is the task confronting introverts while crusaderism is the challenge extroverts must face," Peterson reminds us. He quotes Jungian analyst, Frances Wickes, who outlines the different life tasks for each psychological type:

> The extrovert spending himself freely in relationships and holding himself in continual contact with the world of things and people must learn that we can give only from our wealth, not from our poverty; and realize that without an inner development there may be nothing worth the giv-

> ing or building, for the outer life may become a mass of disconnected fragments.
>
> The introvert, withdrawing constantly into himself, must learn completion through relationships and outer achievement. He must understand that possession without use is also barren and that use in its broader sense involves the connection of the inner and the outer (Peterson, 1992, IFL, p. 39).

We can conclude from the above description that Jung, as an introvert, would approach the meaning Gestalt differently than Frankl, who was rather pragmatic in this treatment approach. With greater understanding comes deeper respect for both. In spite of their different paths, they both seek to return to the same source–whether it is termed *mysterium* or the *noetic dimension*. Both want to anchor themselves and their clients in commitment to *meaning* in life.

☙

Having briefly defined and compared forces or waves in the American Schools of Psychology, and having found a place for Franklian psychology among them, we cannot neglect to take a look at the contemporary scene in practical terms. An interview with someone familiar with numerous aspects and the problems encountered in the delivery of psychotherapy is therefore included here as being relevant for cosideration.

Relevance of Logotherapy in Today's Health Care Climate

With the advent of "managed care" in the US, health care givers in the mental health field are scrambling to find more effective, shorter term, therapeutic approaches. This will also be the case for pastoral psychologists who work in settings where third party payment is accepted. In an article, "Logotherapy in Today's Managed Care Climate" (Graber with Gennari, *The International Forum for Logotherapy*) the author explored these problems with Helen Gennari, who brings 38 years of experience in the mental health field in various positions (social worker, hospital administrator, and case manager for a managed care organization) to the interview. Ms. Gennari is familiar with all sides of the problem, including the vantage point of the patient or client. She describes the challenges she faces as a therapist trying to meet the needs of clients who have a limited number of sessions available to them through their managed care provider. Although more people have insurance coverage for mental health today than in the past, the number of sessions and, therefore, the duration of treatment, is by necessity brief. Excerpts from the published interview will pinpoint the dilemmas faced by caregivers, providers, patients and clients.

Helen: *Many of us are frustrated because we are trying to work in a new framework with old tools. The traditional ways in which we were trained to do psychotherapy are not always easily applicable to the short time frame available to us now. Currently we are trying to use therapies in a framework for which they were not designed. We are looking for better, more effective methods to accomplish our tasks.*

Ann: *With the emphasis in therapy today being on effective short-term care, a remark by Donald Tweedie, Ph.D., comes to mind. He cites a survey of the session frequency of patients seen in Dr. Frankl's clinic* *during a two-year period as slightly less than eight. Also noted by him was the remarkable effectiveness of logotherapy* ("Religious Counseling" [1979]. In Fabry, et al. [Eds.] *Logotherapy in Action*, p. 147). *Are you also seeing logotherapy as that 'more effective method?'*

Helen: *Yes! I think, logotherapy can provide an important part of the answer to the managed care dilemma in mental health. Logotherapy is particularly well suited to fit into the current climate of reaching therapeutic goals. The preferred treatment modality today is* ***brief therapy****. If we look at some of the basic principles of solution-focused brief therapy alongside logotherapy, you will see similarities. The major points of brief therapy are:*

- *It is situation-oriented.*
- *Focus is on client strengths rather than on pathology.*
- *Goal setting is done by the client, not the therapist.*
- *Responsibility for change rests with the client; it's not therapist dependent.*
- *Belief is maintained that all environments, even the most bleak, contain resources.*
- *Interviewing questions are designed to focus on imagining the future when the problem is solved; the kind of questioning that enables the birth of a latent idea.*

These tenets are also inherent in Viktor Frankl's logotherapy. However, logotherapy, with its meaning-seeking motivation–its spiritually-based psychotherapy–can help clients find their noetic goals and build a meaning-filled future. Wouldn't this be far more productive than just acquiring coping skills? And it could probably be accomplished in a shorter period of time, thus reducing the frustrations of all parties.

Ann: *You mean that logotherapy could actually be beneficial to all three: client, managed care organization [health insurance provider], and therapist.*

Helen: *Yes, especially the last. As therapists, we want to assist our clients to discover their own solutions to existing problems. We also want to accomplish this within their available insurance coverage so they can afford the treatment they need.*

Ann: *I can see that you have looked at the problem from everyone's angle.*

Helen: *Indeed I have. That's why I think the time is ripe for logotherapy. You have to make the merits of Franklian psychology and logotherapy widely known. You, who are trained in logotherapy, need to put your heads together to show us, who are on the front lines, how to apply logotherapy in today's climate of care giving.*

Ann: *How do you foresee logotherapy fitting into managed care in the future?*

Helen: *I would like to point out to you that* ***managed care*** *could well be the mechanism through which logotherapy becomes widely used - even if for economic reasons alone. Furthermore, logotherapy's* ***holistic*** *approach of taking body, mind, and the* ***human spirit*** *into consideration in healing is highly acceptable today. That may not have been the case in decades past. Logotherapy could well become the primary treatment modality, where applicable, in the near future* (IFL, 1999, Vol. 22, pp. 27-29).

Since neither pastoral psychologists nor other caregivers are exempt from economic realities, the above was included in this study as being relevant and pertinent for consideration when choosing a treatment method.

X

CONCLUSION

What Works in Psychotherapy

When the bereaved, bewildered, angry, psychologically wounded, spiritually despairing or confused cross our threshold, it is good to know that those who have gone before us in this work have devised a road map we can follow; and, that treatment can be offered with some degree of certainty for therapeutic success if a good map is followed.

After forty years as a clinical psychologist and logotherapist, Dr. James Crumbaugh has seen many trends in psychotherapy come and go. Reflecting on his long and very successful career of helping thousands of patients, he offers his observation of what works in counseling and why it works. Some basic elements have to be present in the treatment protocol in order to be of value and lead to long-term success. In an article, "Logotherapy in the Psychotherapeutic Smorgasbord," (IFL, Vol. 8, 1985, pp. 28-33) he lists and describes the following essential elements:

- Catharsis
- Relationship/Encounter
- Prestige Suggestion
- Reeducation
  [as reorientation through new insights gained]
- Commitment to new goals
  [by carrying out the insights gained].

As demonstrated in the examples of case studies given in the preceding chapters, the therapeutic progression—as identified by Crumbaugh—can be noted. Often beginning with *catharsis*, the process will lead to *reorientation through new insights*, especially noetic insights of discovering meanings waiting to be fulfilled. Then, *commitment* to carry out these meaningful tasks needs to follow. This progression in growth or psycho-spiritual healing is most likely to occur when there is an authentic and caring *therapeutic relationship* between client and pastoral psychologist or someone in that capacity.

Prestige suggestion, Crumbaugh maintains, is an important element initially. In implies to the client that the chosen helper has the necessary competence. This alone reduces client's anxiety. Be it the physician's white coat and black bag, the psychoanalyst's couch, or the clerical collar, these symbols of the trade are perceived as badges of authority for those to whom the client has turned in a time of need. The symbols engender confidence in the distraught who have come to a person or place where help is available. It is suggestive of the prestige of the office or office holder and comforting while the client or patient is dependent on such help.

Following catharsis (as symptoms are reduced, disappear or become bearable), the client can be oriented toward meaningful activities and experiences, and changes in attitude. Logotherapy is ultimately very pragmatic. Existential analysis may give us insights into the problem or situation at hand, but we need to move into commitment to something or someone. Direction needs to be found that will lead to a more fulfilling and meaning-centered future based on the client's highest values. The uniqueness of the individual must always be considered. Activities and experiences will only be healing if they are self-chosen. Orientation toward values to be found in experiences, activities or attitudes will have to reflect the innate talents and qualities of the client–only then will giving them authentic expression be healing.

Some positive changes should be observable fairly soon after the initial encounter between client and therapist. Beyond that, therapy will proceed at the rate of speed at which a client is ready to grow and, at times, how hard the therapist is willing to work. Growth becomes evident in the commitment or dedication to self-chosen meaningful goals, which brings fulfillment. Although there is no guarantee for "therapeutic success," Crumbaugh reminds us that it can at least be said that logotherapy is "on the move." And, when the above process or therapeutic flow is followed, treatment success tends to be lasting (p.33).

Crumbaugh holds that logotherapy is the most direct distillation of what leads to psychotherapeutic success because it incorporates the essential elements he described. Furthermore, it engages the client holistically: physically, psychologically (intellectually and emotionally) and spiritually. It awakens his "will to meaning." For the client who is vitally engaged in his process an awareness of inner strengths, which may have been latent previously, emerges. The client begins to experience himself as the person he may yet become; this is hopeful and expansive. It motivates him to persist and grow beyond his current limitations. Even if he cannot change his outer circumstances, at least, he can change his stance toward them. As he develops more of his latent potential he begins to trust that, even though he may not be exempt from further challenges in the future, he will be able to face them courageously. This minimizes relapse by optimizing inner resources. All of the above are compelling reasons for the efficacy of logotherapy, particularly in basically healthy persons, who are experiencing traumatic events in their lives, and are seeking help from pastoral care or other professionals.

"Therapeutic success" usually indicates that the client is returned to his former baseline functioning. Logotherapy wants more than that. If someone has undergone a serious life crisis or trauma, has not only survived it but shouldered it to the best of his or her ability, should it not have resulted in inner growth that would lead to better than pre-trauma levels of functioning? This is a different measuring rod for "therapeutic success." Yet, for the pastoral psychologist it may be the most valid.

Summary of Study

This treatise began with a brief overview of the historical setting of the birthplace of psychotherapy, Vienna, in the early 1900's. The socio-political atmosphere of Austria, particularly of its capital city, Vienna, was portrayed as the crucible where psychotherapy, the new specialty in the field of human sciences, had its inception and further development. Beginning with Sigmund Freud's *psychoanalysis*, the unfolding of the three Viennese Schools of Psychotherapy was traced through Alfred Adler's *individual psychology* to Viktor Frankl's *existential analysis* and *logotherapy* (Fig. 1). The development of psychotherapy was highlighted against the backdrop of Vienna's cultural, political, and economic milieu during the tumultuous era preceding WW-I to the end of WW-II and its aftermath.

The philosophical roots of Franklian psychology were explored, beginning with classical *Greek philosophy*, through the influences of the *Enlightenment*, leading to *Existentialism* and the *Phenomenology* of Husserl and Scheler. Frankl's place among existential psychologists and phenomenologists was established.

An extensive segment of the study was devoted to examining Frankl's position on *religion* and logotherapy's compatibility with religion. Frankl maintained that religion is a highly personal matter and that views on religion, per se, did not belong in scientific literature. However, even a cursory reading of his work reveals a man of deep faith. The influence of Jewish wisdom literature is evident throughout Frankl's writing and teaching. It may not be explicitly stated, but it is implicit throughout his work. In his autobiographical material he freely talks about his Jewish roots, proudly points to his mother's patrician heritage traceable to prominent rabbis in Prague, reaching back to the late Middle Ages. He movingly describes the sustaining impact of faith in God, his own, as well as faith in God observed in others, particularly in excruciatingly difficult times.

It was found that Frankl's logotherapy is not only open to religion, but that its therapeutic system is based on the recognition of the human spirit as an integral and central part of the human being. This is expressed in Frankl's often extolled maxim, "The medicine chest of the logotherapist lies in the noetic dimension." Therefore, inner strengths residing in the noetic dimension need to be vitally engaged in the therapeutic process in order for lasting transformation, beyond temporary behavioral modification, to occur. Whether rooted in Jewish mysticism or the verities of perennial philosophy, logotherapy's *ecumenical posture* and its consequent efficacy for counseling persons of various religious persuasions became apparent.

The major tenets of logotheory: (1) *Freedom of Will*; (2) *Will to Meaning*; (3) *Meaning of Life* were presented as the fundamental philosophical assumptions upon which Frankl's therapeutic system is based. The wide cross-cultural appeal of the above premises, further expressed in his therapeutic approach, was noted. The very intent of logotherapy is inclusive and well suited for transprofessional, crosscultural, and interfaith dialogue. Frankl's strongest statement on how the human race is divided was found in this comment, "There are only two races of men: the decent and the unprincipled. And they can be found among all peoples."

Frankl's *dimensional ontology* (Fig. 2) was explained at length culminating in a *wholeness model of integrated dimensions* (Fig. 3). In their dimensional relatedness these models analogously attempt to depict the human being in her/his entirety. The exclusion of any one of them, particularly the exclusion of the dimension of the human spirit (which is largely still done in many psychotherapeutic modalities), constitutes a reductionistic view and treatment of the human being. The spiritual dimension—being innermost—is also perceived to be the most inclusive. The search for meaning was seen as the journey to the spiritual or noetic center, the nucleus of personality, where the *Logos* (meaning) is encountered.

According to logotherapy, meaning is experienced on two levels: *ultimate meaning* and *meaning of the moment*. The first, ultimate meaning, is found through participation in a universal order of being in which every person has a place. To this genus of meaning questions, such as, "Who am I?" are addressed. Ultimate meaning can never be comprehended in its entirety, only pursued to the best of one's ability. The second, meaning of the moment, is much easier to grasp. In most situations it is nothing spectacular, just the daily tasks awaiting us. Some moments offer bigger choices than others; some moments are subtler than others; none are repeatable.

Ways to discover meaning that enable a person to live responsibly were seen as being available through three avenues:

1) **Creativity**: by creating a work or accomplishing a task.
2) **Experience**: by experiencing something in life (such as goodness, truth or beauty), or by encountering another person in the unique quality of the other's existence, through love.

3) **Attitude**: by the attitude a person brings toward life situations, particularly the stance taken in unavoidable suffering.

The instrument, *Reflections of the Meaning Triangle* (Fig. 5), served as a strengths awareness tool. It helped to bring creative, experiential, and attitudinal values to conscious awareness and aided in clarifying values that are important to a client. In keeping with logotherapy's emphasis on "what's right about you," and by deemphasizing "what's wrong with you," it can serve as a starting point for the therapeutic process.

Among the fundamental treatment premises particular importance was placed on the principle of *noodynamic* tension, which states: in the physical dimension homeostasis or balance is necessary; in the psychological dimension, it is usually desirable; but, in the noetic or spiritual dimension it is deadly! It leads to stagnation and stifles growth, leading to apathy and resulting in inertia. Noodynamic (spirit activated) tension is needed to move us forward. This is an area where logotherapy departs from most other counseling theories, which advocate homeostasis on all levels.

Frankl's summary of the human condition—as experienced in Life, Death, Suffering, Work, Love—narrowed the field of myriad presenting problems into these five general areas. Questions and dilemmas arising when meaning in any of these areas cannot be found were seen as most likely to be encountered by pastoral psychologists. A note of caution that the pathology of mental illness is the domain of psychiatry, and not of pastoral psychology, was sounded.

The application of logotherapy in key areas of human suffering was carefully delineated with attention given to the general domain belonging to pastoral psychology (Fig. 6). Into that domain belong such human sufferings as:

- **Despondency:** Expressed in pain, guilt, and death, which comprises the ***tragic triad***.
- **Despair:** Giving rise to depression, aggression, and addiction, which constitutes the the ***neurotic triad***.
- **Doubt and Confusion:** Often caused by an inner emptiness when access to the noetic dimension or one's spiritual core is blocked, is experienced as ***existential vacuum***.

The above named conditions represent the underlying dynamics that will present symptomatically as a wide range of human problems that will bring suffering people to the doors of pastoral psychologists and other therapists. A long list of presenting problems was included in Chapter Three. Upon closer scrutiny, it can be readily seen that most human anguish arises from the five general areas outlined by Frankl (meaning of life, death, suffering, work, love) and has *despondency, despair, doubts and confusion* as its etiology, which needs to be dealt with for lasting change to occur.

Vital elements in logotherapeutic treatment planning were outlined, such as: Distancing from symptoms, modification of attitudes, reduction of symptoms, and orientation toward meaningful goals. The wisdom of *prevention* and *postvention* was emphasized. Areas of special interest to pastoral psychology were addressed, such as *comforting* where cure is not possible, and *pastoral trauma intervention*. "Pitfalls to avoid" cautioned against inducing *ecclesiogenic damage* by playing God!

A chart of the American Schools of Psychology (Fig. 7) presented a brief overview of the various *forces* or *waves* in psychology among the American schools of psychological theories. Begining with the *First Force* (Psychoanalysis), leading to the *Second Force* (Behaviorism), Frankl's logotherapy was positioned in that chart and found to be an ideal bridge between the *Third Force*

(Existential-Humanistic Psychology), and the emerging *Fourth Force* (Transpersonal Psychology). A comparison between the philosophical and psychological postulates of William James, an advanced thinker far ahead of his time, and Viktor Frankl showed great similarity in their Gedankengut or perceptiveness.

Similarly, a comparison of Viktor Frankl with another psychotherapist who is highly regarded in pastoral psychology, Carl Gustav Jung, was undertaken. Although vastly different in their treatment approaches, their agreement on spirit—as a vital resource in therapy—was seen as the entree to pastoral psychology they hold in common. Meaning orientation, anchored commitment, and the high value placed on responsibility are other common elements in their counseling theories (Fig. 8).

Lastly, excerpts from a published interview, "Logotherapy in Today's Managed Care Climate," which the author conducted with Helen Gennari, shed light on the economic reality of psychotherapy and the availability of mental health care. The inclusion of that material was deemed relevant in today's managed care climate in the U.S.

The conclusion attempted to answer the question that every practitioner yielding a new tool secretly wonders about, namely, "Does it work?" A seasoned professional, Dr. Crumbaugh, offered his observations of what works in psychotherapy and why it works. After working with, and even crafting some of the "tools of the trade" during forty years in practice, he tells us with conviction that some elements are essential to the treatment protocol to bring about therapeutic success. He lists the following as being indispensable: catharsis, relationship/encounter, prestige suggestion, reeducation toward meaning goals, and commitment to new goals. Musing over the "psychotherapeutic smorgasboard" of available offerings, he holds that logotherapy is the most direct distillation of treatment approaches that work because it incorporates all of the essential elements. In addition, it awakens clients' "Will to Meaning" and engages them holistically—inclusive of the human spirit.

Coming from a giant in his field, someone with his lengths and breadth of clinical experience, Dr. Crumbaugh's assessment and endorsement of Viktor Frankl's logotherapy sounds a hopeful note for its future.

Viktor Frankl's Logotherapy as Method of Choice in Ecumenical Pastoral Psychology

The stated objective of this study was to do a scholarly search and compilation of the work of Viktor Emil Frankl, M.D., Ph.D., in the English and German repertoire, to ascertain whether Viktor Frankl's logotherapy was the method of choice for pastoral psychology, where applicable.

In view of the foregoing summary of the exhaustive research of Franklian theory and its application in practice, it is the author's contention that the stated objective—to ascertain that Viktor Frankl's logotherapy is the optimal choice in ecumenical pastoral psychology—has been accomplished. The criteria for that assertion are:

- Logotherapy with the inclusion of the spiritual dimension in its treatment model, its meaning-seeking approach, and its orientation to responsibility, is ideologically ideally suited to pastoral psychology.
- Logotherapy has the inherent facility for intervention in common life crises. Logotherapy deals pragmatically with problems of clients by utilizing available strengths and inner resources to shape a healthier future. This is of particular interest to professionals working with cur-

rent difficulties, sometimes of crisis proportions, usually on a short-time basis.

- A further aspiration of this work was to present treatment tools usable by pastoral psychologists, which are spiritually based and psychologically sound. This aspiration was met through the presentation of therapeutic techniques developed or adapted by Dr. Frankl and other logotherapists. The major established techniques for intervention described and demonstrated were: *Self-distancing* or *Self-detachment*, *Paradoxical Intention*, *Socratic Dialogue* with its maieutic questioning, and *Dereflection*. Stellar examples of further developments in logotherapy were highlighted from works by James Crumbaugh, Joseph Fabry, Elisabeth Lukas, Paul Welter, and others.
- *The Rogina Model for Treating Violent Behaviors* addressed violence and its underlying despair (manifesting as a noogenic neurosis or deficiency) that will be "cured" when the human spirit is willing to participate in the process of change.
- Also introduced was the strengths awareness instrument, *Reflections on the Meaning Triangle*; and, a specific treatment tool, *The Logoanchor Technique*, with pertinent examples of its wide application potential demonstrated.
- Finally, the use of any method common to the psychotherapeutic repertoire, which is compatible with the spirit of logotherapy, was encouraged. Logotherapy was found to be open to other systems of psychotherapy as well as to its own expansion.

☙

The efficacy of ***Viktor Frankl's Logotherapy as Method of Choice in Ecumenical Pastoral Psychology*** was further illustrated through the inclusion of existential/phenomenological material in the following examples and case studies:

- *We noted the insightful responses of numerous persons (pointing to an awareness of their strengths) in the instrument,* ***Reflections on the Meaning Triangle****.*
- *We observed Lucy's valiant struggle through the pain, guilt, and loss of giving up her baby at birth, to overcome her* ***despondency****, heal the past, and courageously embark upon a teaching career.*
- *We experienced Katie's* ***despair*** *and anguish that brought on suicidal ideations. We saw her rising above her self-absorption, finding a meaningful goal for her future, and accepting her unalterable fate.*
- *We saw Fr. Joseph's* ***existential vacuum*** *lift when he found his way back to God by expressing his creativity through painting; finding inner peace, and voicing a readiness to die.*
- *We agonized with LK's* ***traumatic experience*** *of having to identify the mutilated remains of her twin sister, and witnessed how she derived comfort from her faith and her belief in an afterlife; and, how she was instrumental in helping her parents deal with their loss.*
- *In an interview H. Gennari's voice of experience pointed to logotherapy as being optimally suited to meet the contemporary demands for a* ***holistic approach to psychotherapy****, as well as the economic realities of managed health care.*
- *Finally, Dr. Crumbaugh, based on his research and experience with thousands of patients over the years, found logotherapy to be the premier tool to help suffering persons* ***find meaning and purpose in life****.*

ꕥ

As demonstrated in the case presentations, logotherapy served as the intervention of choice when basically healthy and normally functioning persons experienced difficulties that went beyond their ability to cope. When people find themselves unable to continue their life journey at a previous level of functioning or coping, those are the times when the help of pastoral psychologists or other helpers will be sought.

Because logotherapy believes that each person is unique and has the answers to his life challenges deep within, it becomes the helper's task to bring out this latent knowing. This belief carries with it the trust that the potential to face and to overcome existential difficulties is also present. The suffering person is pointed to the *Logos* within; thereby he is brought in touch with his highest values and his own inner strengths and resources. The responsibility to implement them is the client's, not the counselor's.

Logotherapy is eager to assist people to stand in their own strength, to be self-dependent by being noetically anchored, and NOT to become therapist dependent. Since logotherapy's role as a psychotherapy ends when the client regains well-being, clients are encouraged to continue their spiritual journey in their own faith tradition.

ꕥ

Final Remarks by Viktor Frankl

Logotherapy states that man should not ask what the meaning of life is, but rather, must recognize that it is *he* who is being asked. *Life* is the questioner. Man must respond to life by courageously facing and responsibly carrying out the demands life places before him—thereby he finds fulfillment in life while living his vocation of destiny.

It is deemed best to let Viktor Frankl himself have the final word in this study. In his last and, by his own admission, favorite book, *Man's Search for Ultimate Meaning* (1997), we read, "As to logotherapy, it is not a panacea." He advises that logotherapy, therefore, is open to cooperation with other approaches to psychotherapy; it is open to its own evolution; and, it is open to religion. This is indispensable: Logotherapy deals with the *Logos*—with meaning. Dr. Frankl concludes by stating, "Specifically, I see the meaning of logotherapy in helping others to see meaning in life." (p. 136).

ღ

APPENDIX A

GLOSSARY of LOGOTHERAPEUTIC TERMS and PHRASES

CONSCIENCE – "is that capacity which empowers [a person] to seize the meaning of a situation in its very uniqueness" (Frankl, 1969/1988, p. 19). "So meaning must be found and cannot be given. And it must be found by oneself, by one's own conscience. Conscience may be defined as a means to discover meanings, to 'sniff them out,' as it were. In fact, conscience lets us arrive at the unique meaning gestalts dormant in all the unique situations which form a string called a man's life" (Frankl, 1975, p. 115).

DEREFLECTION – Focusing attention away from the situation. It rests "...on two essential qualities of human existence, namely, man's capacities of self-transcendence and self-detachment" (Frankl, 1969/1988, p 99). "The essence of dereflection is substituting something positive for something negative... When turning toward a new interest is successful or is rewarded, turning from intense self-observation is more likely to succeed" (Lukas, 1984, p. 40).

ECCLESIOGENIC DAMAGE – Damage caused by the clergy (Frankl, 1969/1988, pp. 131-132).

EXISTENTIAL – "...may be used in three ways: to refer to (a) existence itself, i.e., the specifically human mode of being; (b) the meaning of existence; and (c) the striving to find a concrete meaning in personal existence, that is to say, the will to meaning" (Frankl, 1963/1977, p. 159).

EXISTENTIAL ANALYSIS *(GENERAL)* – Psychotherapy whose starting-point and whose particular concern is making man conscious of his responsibility. It is the "...analysis of the responsibility aspects of being human" (Frankl, 1955, p. 72).

EXISTENTIAL ANALYSIS *(SPECIAL)* – "Insofar as existential analysis by definition is analysis of human existence in terms of responsibility, special existential analysis is analysis of psychic illness in terms of responsibility" (Frankl, 1955, p. 201).

EXISTENTIAL FRUSTRATION – "...frustration of the will-to-meaning (which) may lead to neurosis" (Frankl, 1955, p. xi). "It is in itself neither pathological nor pathogenic. A man's concern, even his despair, over the worthwhileness of life is a spiritual distress but by no means a mental disease (Frankl, 1963/1977, p. 163).

EXISTENTIAL NEUROSIS – As opposed to a clinical neurosis, it is a "sense of despair over the meaning of life" (Frankl, 1955, p. xi).

EXISTENTIAL VACUUM – A general sense of meaninglessness and emptiness, an "inner void," an "abyss-experience" (Frankl, 1969/1988, p. 83). "[It] manifests itself mainly in a state of boredom" (Frankl, 1963/1977, p. 169). "No instinct tells him what he has to do, and no tradition tells him what he ought to do: soon he will not know what he wants to do. More and more he will be governed by what others want him to do, thus increasingly falling prey to conformism" (Frankl, 1963/1977, p. 168).

FATE – is "what lies beyond human freedom—beyond our power and responsibility. Fate is the totality of all determining factors. But it is also the springboard of our freedom—the challenge to respond to fate (in contrast to animals) in various ways, and (again in contrast to animals) to be response-able for our choices. Fate, for Frankl, is not the cause of human thoughts and actions but their precondition. It does not explain our reactions but triggers them. Fate makes us human because it forces us to choose among the available potentialities, and thus to make use of our human freedom" (Lukas, 1986, p. 20).

FREEDOM – "...is a word often misused. To avoid misunderstandings, Frankl does not speak of freedom from something, especially not from conditions (no one is free from his or her physical and psychological conditions). Frankl speaks of freedom to something—a freely taken attitude toward these conditions. He stresses the attitude of 'despite,' our choice of response to fate" (Lukas, 1986, p. 19).

HOMEOSTASIS – "This principle, in various forms, holds that we have all sorts of needs that push us toward gratification of those needs. Unless they are gratified, our inner equilibrium is thrown off and we become sick or abnormal. The homeostasis principle is true for animals and also for infants whose dimension of the spirit exists only as potential. The baby cries when hungry, sleeps contentedly when full. The more the human spirit develops, the more the homeostasis principle loses validity; the goal is no longer simple gratification of needs, short-range pleasure, abreaction of drives, and the whole range of motivational theories...If there is freedom in choosing attitudes, we can also choose whether want gratification. We can say 'no' to gratification without being considered sick or abnormal" (Lukas, 1986, p. 2 1-22).

HUMAN EXISTENCE – is characterized by three factors: "man's spirituality, his freedom, his responsibility" (Frankl, 1955, p. xviii). "Logotherapy's concept of man is based on three pillars, the freedom of will, the will to meaning, and the meaning of life" (Frankl, 1969/1988, p. 16).

HYPERINTENTION – Attempts to escape the **EXISTENTIAL VACUUM** by focusing on the pursuit of pleasure. The direct intention on pleasure defeats itself. "The more an individual aims at pleasure, the more he misses the aim" (Frankl, 1969/1988, p 100).

HYPERREFLECTION – Excessive attention. "Spontaneity and activity are impeded if made a target of too much attention" (Frankl, 1969/1988, p 100).

IATROGENIC DAMAGE – Damage caused by the doctor or therapist.

LOGOS – is a Greek word that denotes "meaning" and "spirit" (Frankl, 1963/1 977, p. 160).

LOGOTHERAPY – "focuses on the meaning of human existence as well as on man's search for such a meaning. According to logotherapy, the striving to find a meaning in one's life is the primary motivational force in man" (Frankl, 1963/1977, p. 154). It is "...a psychotherapy which not only recognizes man's spirit, but actually starts from it" (Frankl, 1955, p. xi).

LOGOTHERAPIST'S ROLE – "...consists in widening and broadening the visual field of the client so that the whole spectrum of meaning and values becomes conscious and visible to him" (Frankl, 1963/1977, p. 174). "The aim of the psychotherapist should be to bring out the ultimate possibilities in the patient. Not to penetrate his deepest secrets, but to realize his latent values—remembering the aphorism of Goethe, which might well be adopted as the maxim of psychotherapy: 'If we take people as they are, we make them worse. If we treat them as if they were what they ought to be, we help them to become what they are capable of becoming" (Frankl, 1955, p. 9).

MEANING OF LIFE – Differing from person to person, from day to day, and from hour to hour, the specific meaning of a person's life at a given moment (Frankl, 1963/1977, p. 171).

a. Frankl had a strong conviction that "Despite the crumbling of traditions, life holds a meaning for each and every individual, and even more, it retains this meaning literally to his last breath" (Frankl, 1969/1988, p. ix).
b. The therapist "cannot show his client what the meaning is, but he may well show him that there is a meaning, and that life retains it: that remains meaningful under any conditions" (Frankl, 1969/1988, p. ix).
c. "The meaning of life is neither reachable nor unreachable, not repeatable or replaceable. The meaning of life lies in its pursuit" (Lukas, 1986, p. 79).

MEANING OF LIFE *(THE DISCOVERY OF)* – According to Logotherapy, one can discover this meaning in life in three primary ways:

a. in creative action—by doing a deed—*Realizing Creative Values* (Frankl, 1955, p. 49);
b. in passively experiencing the Good, the True, and the Beautiful—*Realizing Experiential Values* (Frankl, 1955, p. xii);
c. in suffering, when life is neither fruitful in creation nor rich in experience—by one's attitude to an unalterable fate—*Realizing Attitudinal Values* (Frankl, 1955, p. 50). "The right kind of suffering—facing your fate without flinching—is the highest achievement that has been granted to man" (Frankl, 1955, p. xii).

MEANING OF LOVE – "Love is the only way to grasp another human being in the innermost core of his or her personality...By the spiritual act of love he is enabled to see the essential traits and features in the beloved person; and even more, he sees that which is potential in him, that which has not yet actualized... Furthermore, by his love, the loving person enables the beloved person to actualize the potentialities" (Frankl, 1963/1977, p. 176-177).

MEANING OF SUFFERING – "When one is confronted with an inescapable, unavoidable situation, whenever one has to face a fate that cannot be changed, e.g., an incurable disease, just then is one given a last chance to actualize the highest values, to fulfill the deepest meaning, the meaning of suffering" (Frankl, 1963/1977, p. 178).

NOETIC – adj. Pertaining to or originating in the nous (Greek: mind).

NOETIC DIMENSION – The dimension of the human spirit containing our healthy core, where can be found such uniquely human attributes as: will to meaning, ideas and ideals, creativity, imagination, faith, love, conscience, self-detachment, self-transcendence, humor, striving toward goals, and taking on commitments and responsibilities. The logotherapist mobilizes these innate human qualities in therapy.

NOÖ-DYNAMICS – "...a tension between what one has already achieved and what one still ought to accomplish, or the gap between what one is and what one should become...What man needs is not a tensionless state but rather the striving and struggling for some goal worthy of him... Noö-dynamics are "...the spiritual dynamics in a polar field of tension where one pole is represented by a meaning to be fulfilled and the other pole by the man who must fulfill it" "...frustration of the will-to-meaning (which) may lead to neurosis" (Frankl, 1963/1977, pp. 164-166).

NOÖGENIC – A logotherapeutic term which refers to anything having to do with the "spiritual" core of one's personality. It is important to keep in mind that the word "spiritual," within the frame of reference of logotherapy, does not mean "religious" but instead it refers to the specifically human dimension of human beings. "Noetic phenomena" would be a dimension above somatic and psychic phenomena.

NOÖGENIC NEUROSES – Neuroses which "...do not emerge from conflicts between drives and instincts but from conflicts between various values; in other words moral conflicts or from spiritual problems" (Frankl, 1963/1977, p. 160). It is defined as "...a neurosis which is caused by a spiritual problem, a moral or ethical conflict, as for example, a conflict between the mere superego and the true conscience" (Frankl, 1969/1988, p. 89).

PAN-DETERMINISM – "...a dangerous assumption...the view of man that disregards his capacity to take a stand toward any conditions whatsoever. Man is not fully conditioned and determined; he determines himself whether to give in to conditions or stand up to them. In other words, man is ultimately self-determining" (Frankl, 1963/1977, p. 206).

PARADOXICAL INTENTION – "...means that the patient is encouraged to do, or wish to happen, the very things he fears" (Frankl, 1969/1988, p 102). It "...lends itself to the short-term treatment of obsessive-compulsive and phobic patients" (Frankl, 1969/1988, p. 101). "Paradoxical Intention is a wish turned upside down. Patients are guided to wish exactly what as phobics and obsessives they have so frantically feared and so desperately tried to avoid. What we flee from tends to catch up with us, and the more we fight a fear the more we become its victims. On the other hand, if we wish to have happen what we fear and support our paradoxical wish with humoristically exaggerated formulations, the fear dissolves" (Lukas, 1984, p. 36).

REDUCTIONISM – "...a pseudoscientific approach which disregards and ignores the humanness of phenomena by making them into mere epiphenomena, more specifically, by reducing them to subhuman phenomena...one could define reductionism as subhumanism (Frankl, 1969/1988, p. 18).

SELF-DETACHMENT – "By virtue of this capacity man is capable of detaching himself not only from a situation but also from himself. He is capable of choosing his attitude toward himself. By so doing he really takes a stand toward his own somatic and psychic conditions and determinants" (Frankl, 1969/1988, p. 17). (See "Dereflection.") (Sometimes called "self-distancing"; see Lukas, 1984, p. 36): "Self-distancing is the capacity to step away from ourselves and to look at ourselves from the 'outside,' possibly with humor."

SELF-TRANSCENDENCE – "Self-transcendence is our ability to reach beyond ourselves to people we love or to causes that are important to us" (Lukas, 1984, p. 34). "Human existence is essentially self-transcendence rather than self-actualization. Self-actualization is not a possible aim at all, for the simple reason that the more a man would strive for it, the more he would miss it. For only to the extent to which man commits himself to the fulfillment of his life's meaning, to this extent he also actualizes himself. In other words, self-actualization cannot be attained if it is made an end in itself, but only as a side effect of self-transcendence" (Frankl, 1963/1977, p. 175). "Self-transcendence is the essence of existence. Being human is being directed to something other than itself" (Frankl, 1969/1988, p. 50).

SUPRA-MEANING – The ultimate meaning which "...necessarily exceeds and surpasses the finite intellectual capacities of man" (Frankl, 1963/1977, p. 187).

VALUES – "...do not drive a man; they do not push him, but rather pull him" (Frankl, 1963/1977, p. 157) "...one may define values as those meaning universals which crystallize in the typical situations a society or even humanity has to face" (Frankl, 1969/1988, p. 56).

WILL-TO-MEANING – "According to logotherapy, the striving to find a meaning in one's life is the primary motivational force in man." This is in opposition to the pleasure principle or "will-to-pleasure" of Freud, and the "will-to-power" stressed by Adler (Frankl, 1963/1977, p. 154).

☙

The author gratefully acknowledges that the foregoing "Glossary of Logotherapeutic Terms and Phrases" was compiled by George E. Naff and used with his kind permission.

REFERENCES

Barnes, R. C. (1994). *Introduction to Viktor Frankl's logotherapy.* (Available from: Viktor Frankl Institute of Logotherapy. Abilene, TX)

Corsini, Raymond (1999). *Dictionary of psychology.* Philadelphia, PA: Brunner-Mazel.

Cooper, D. E. (1990). *Existentialism: A reconstruction.* Oxford, UK and Cambridge, MA: Blackwell.

Cousins, E. H. (1983). "World spirituality: An encyclopedic history of the religious quest." *Crossroads/Continuum Bulletin.* New York: Continuum.

Crumbaugh, J. & Maholick L. (1969/1981). Purpose in Life Test. *Manual of instruction* (Manual #168). Murfreesboro, TN: Phychometric Affiliates.

Crumbaugh, J. (1985). Logotherapy in the Psychotherapeutic Smorgasbord.
International Forum for Logotherapy, 28-33. Abilene, TX: Viktor Frankl Institute of Logotherapy.

Decker, H. S. "Adler, Alfred," *World Book Online Americas Edition.* Retrieved: 10/3/2001 at: Http://www.aolsvc.worldbook.aol.com/wbol/wbPage/na/ar/co/004760

Decker, H. S. "Freud, Sigmund," *World Book Online - Americas Edition.* Retrieved: 10/3/2001 at: Http://www.aolsvc.worldbook.aol.com/wbol/wbPage/na/ar/co/211480

Fabry. J. B. (1968/1980/1987/1994). *The pursuit of meaning.* Berkeley, CA: Institute of Logotherapy Press.

Fabry, J. B., Bulka, R. P., Sahakian, W. S. (Eds.), (1979). *Logotherapy in action.* New York: Jason Aronson, Inc.

Fabry, J. B. (1988). *Guideposts to meaning.* Oakland, CA: New Harbinger Publications.

Fabry, J. B. (1993). Joe Fabry letter to President Clinton. In *The International Forum for Logotherapy, 16,* 42. Abilene, TX: Viktor Frankl Institute of Logotherapy.

Frankl, V. E. (1945/1999). *Synchronization in Birkenwald.* (Available on video tape with English subtitles from the Viktor Frankl Institute of Logotherapy, Abilene, TX)

Frankl, V. E. (1959). *From death-camp to existentialism.* Boston, MA: Beacon Press, Beacon Hill.

Frankl, V. E. (1959/1967/1985). *Man's search for meaning.* New York: Washing Square Press.

Frankl, V. E. (1948/1975/1985). *The unconscious God.* New York: Washing Square Press.

Frankl, V. E. (1967/1985). *Psychotherapy and existentialism.* New York: Washing Square Press.

Frankl, V. E. (1986). *The doctor and the soul* (Revised and expanded edition). New York: Vintage Books

Frankl, V. E. (1969/1988). *The will to meaning.* New York: Meridian.

Frankl, V. E. (1997). *Viktor Frankl recollections: An autobiography.* New York and London: Plenum Press.

Frankl, V. E. (1997). *Man's search for ultimate meaning.* New York and London: Plenum Press.

Frankl, V. E. (2001), "Viktor Frankl", *Chronology and Extensive Curriculum Vitae.* Retrieved: October 7, 2001, at: Http://logotherapy.univie.ac.at

Frings, M. S. (1997/2000). "Max Scheler", *Professor Frings' Max Scheler Web Site.* Retrieved: October 11, 2001, at: Http://www.maxscheler.com/Scheler2.htm

Gould, W. B. (1993). *Viktor Frankl - Life with meaning.* Pacific Grove, CA: Brooks/Cole Publishing Company.

Graber, A. V. (1993). "The Logoanchor Technique." *The International Forum for Logotherapy, 16,* 26-30. Abilene, TX: Viktor Frankl Institute of Logotherapy.

Graber, A. V., & Gennari, H. (1999). "Logotherapy in today's manged care climate." *The International Forum for Logotherapy*, 22, 27-30. Abilene, TX: Viktor Frankl Institute of Logotherapy.

Graber, A., & Rogina J. (2001). *Logotherapeutic model of mental health.* (Course Guide; available from the Viktor Frankl Institute of Logotherapy, Abilene, TX).

Guignon, C, & Pereboom, D. (Eds.) (1995). *Existentialism basic writings: Kierkegaard, Nietzsche, Heidegger, Sarte.* Indianapolis, IN: Hackett Publishing Co., Inc.

Huffman, C. "Socrates," *World Book Online Edition.* Retrieved: 10/8/01 at: Http://www.aolsvc.worldbook.aol.com/wbol/wbPage/na/ar/co/518000.

Jung, C. G. (1933). *Modern man in search of a soul.* New York: Harcourt, Brace & World.

Jung, C. G. (1964). *Man and his symbols.* Garden City, NY: Doubleday.

Kalmar, S. (1982). A brief history of logotherapy. In Sandra A. Wawrytko (Ed.),_*Analecta Frankliana.* Berkeley, CA: Institute of Logotherapy Press.

Kok, J. R. & Jongsma, A. E., Jr. (1998). *The pastoral counseling treatment planner.* New York: John Wiley & Sons, Inc.

Kushner, H. (1997). In V. E. Frankl's, *Man's search for ultimate meaning.* New York and London: Plenum Press.

Leslie, R. (1995). "Logotherapy and religion." In *The International Forum for Logotherapy*, 18, 34-35. Abilene, TX: Viktor Frankl Institute of Logotherapy.

Lukas, E. (1979). "The four steps of logotherapy." In J. Fabry, R. Bulka, and W. Sahakian, (Eds.) *Logotherapy in action.*) New York: Jason Aronson.

Lukas, E. (1984). *Meaningful living: A logotherapy guide to health.* New York: Grove Press, Inc.

Lukas, E. (1986). *Meaning in suffering.* Berkely, CA: Institute of Logotherapy Press.

Lukas, E. (1989). *Logotherapy in crisis intervention* (handouts and author's lecture notes from seminar offered in Kansas City, MO)

Lukas, E. (2000). *Logotherapy textbook.* Toronto, Canada: Liberty Press.

May, R. (Ed.) (1969). *Existential psychology,* 2nd ed. New York: Random House.

McGrath, W. J. "Austria," *World Book Online Edition.* Retrieved: 10/13/01 at: Http://www.aolsvc.worldbook.aol.com/wbol/wbPage/na/ar/co/038580

Microsoft, Inc. (1996). *Encarta Encyclopedia.* "Carl Gustav Jung."

Morgan, J. H. (1987). *From Freud to Frankl: Our modern search for personal meaning.* Lima, OH: Windham Hall Press.

Pasco, K. A. (1996). *Processes utilized by chaplains in pastoral care interactions.* Unpublished Doctoral Candidacy Paper, University of Houston, Texas.

Peterson, T. (1992) "Frankl and Jung on Meaning." *The International Forum for Logotherapy, 15,* pp. 33-40. Abilene, TX: Viktor Frankl Institute of Logotherapy.

Popielski, K. (1982). "A general concept of humanity and its meaning for psychotherapy: The anthropological philosophy of Karol Wojtyla and the concept of human nature in V. E. Frankl." In J. Fabry, R. Bulka, and W. Sahakian, (Eds.) *Logotherapy in action.*) New York: Jason Aronson.

Ranier, T. A. (Project Editor). (1997). *The Reader's Digest Illustrated Great World Atlas.* Pleasantville, NY: Reader's Digest.

Rice, G. (Project Chair; Contributors: A. Graber, M. Pitts, J. Rogina, I. Sjolie). (2002). *Viktor Frankl's Logotherapy: Meaning-centered interventions.* (Available from Viktor Frankl Institute of Logotherapy, Abilene, TX)

Rogina, J. (2001) "The Rogina model for treating violent behaviors." In *Logotherapeutic model of mental health.* (Course guide: available from the Viktor Frankl Institute of Logotherapy, Abilene, TX)

Russell, B. (1945). *A history of Western philosophy*. New York: Simon and Schuster.

Sahakian, W. (1979). Logotherapy's Place in Philosophy. In J. Fabry, R. Bulka, & W. Sahakian, (Eds.) *Logotherapy in action*. New York: Jason Aronson.

Seidl, M. (1996). *Die Kunst, sinnvoll zu leben.* Tübingen: Verlag Lebenskunst.

Shinn, R. (1968). *The restless adventure: Essays on contemporary expressions of existentialism.* New York: Scribner's.

Smith, H. (1991). *The world's religions.* San Fransicco: Harper.

Soll, I. "Aristotle," *World Book Online Americas Edition.* Retrieved: 10/8/01 at: Http://www/aolsvc.worldbook.aol.com/wbol/wbPage/na/ar/co/029880.

Soll, I. "Plato," *World Book Online Americas Edition.* Retrieved: 10/8/01 at: Http://www/aolsvc.worldbook.aol.com/wbol/wbPage/na/ar/co/434320.

Soll, I. "Existentialism," *World Book Online Americas Edition.* Retrieved: 10/9/01 at: Http://www.aolsvc.worldbook.aol.com/wbol/wbPage/na/ar/co/188480

Tweedie, D. F. (1979). "Religious Counseling." In J. Fabry, R. Bulka, and W. Sahakian, (Eds.) *Logotherapy in action.* New York: Jason Aronson.

Welter, P. R. (1995). *Franklian psychology and logotherapy* (Available from the Viktor Frankl Institute of Logotherapy, Abilene, TX).

Yoder, J. D. (1989). *Meaning in therapy: A logotherapy casebook.* Columbus, GA: Quill Publications.

BIBLIOGRAPHY

Bucke, Maurice B. (1901/1922/1923). *Cosmic Consciousness.* New York: E. P. Dutton.

Coelho, Mary Conrow. (2002) *Awakening Universe, Emerging Personhood.* Lima, OH: Wyndham Hall Press.

Colman, Andrew M. (2001). *Oxford Dictionary of Psychology.* Oxford University Press, NY.

Corsini, Raymond J. (1999). *The Dictionary of Psychology.* Philadelphia, PA: Brunner/Mazel * Taylor and Francis Group.

Cousins, Ewert H. (1992). *Christ of the 21st Century.* Rockport, MA: Element, Inc.

Craighead, W. E., Nemeroff, C.B., (Eds.) (2001). *The Corsini Encyclopedia of Psychology and Behavior Science* (Third Edition). New York: John Wiley and Sons

Dalai Lama, The. (1999). *Ethics for a New Millennium.* New York: Riverhead Books.

De Mello, Anthony. (1990). *Awareness.* New York: Doubleday.

Frankl, Viktor. (1978) *The Unheard Cry for Meaning.* New York: Simon and Schuster, Inc.

Frankl, Viktor. (1984). *Bewältigung der Vergänglichkeit* (audio cassette). Innsbruck, Austria: Audiotex International.

Frankl, Viktor. (1985). *Re-humanization of Psychotherapy.* Video taped at the University of Texas, Houston. Available from: Viktor Frankl Institute of Logotherapy.

Frankl, Viktor. (1992). *Malone: A Conversation with Viktor Frankl.* Video taped at KTEHSA, San Jose, CA. Available from: Viktor Frankl Institute of Logotherapy.

Frankl, Viktor. (2001). *Chronology, Extensive curriculum vitae.* Retrieved: October 3, 2001, Viktor Frankl Institute, Vienna, at: http://logotherapy.univie.ac.at/indexE.html

Frankl, Viktor. (1956). *Theorie und Therapie der Neurosen.* (Audio cassettes available from: Auditorium Netzwerk) at: http://www.auditorium-netzwerk.de/container_audit.htm

Fox, Matthew & Sheldrake, Rupert (1996). *Natural Grace.* New York: Doubleday.

Gardner, Howard. (1983). *Frames of Mind.* New York: Basic Books

Gibran, Kahlil. (1970). *The Prophet.* New York: Alfred A. Knopf.

Goethe, Johann Wolfgang. (1949). *Trost bei Goethe.* Wien, Austria: Walther Scheuermann Verlag.

Goleman, Daniel. (1995). *Emotional Intelligence.* New York: Bantam Books

Graber, A. & Madsen, M. (1995) *Images of Transformation* (Audio cassette album) Rochester, MI: Fountain Publishing.

Houston, Jean. ((1982). *The Possible Human.* New York: Tarcher/Putnam.

Huxley, Aldous. (1945). *Perennial Philosophy.* New York: Harper and Row.

James, William. (1961/1974). *Varieties of Religious Experience.* New York: Collier Books.

Keller, Helen (Revised and edited by Ray Silverman). (1994). *Light in my Darkness.* West Chester, PA: Chrysalis Books.

Koenig, Harold G. (1999). *The Healing Power of Faith.* New York: Simon and Schuster.

Lent, Timothy. (2002). *Christian Themes in Logotherapy.* Haverford, PA: Infinity Publishing Co.

Malone, Michael (1991). *A Conversation with Viktor Frankl.* Videotape. (KTEHSA, San Hose, Public Television). (Available from Viktor Frankl Institute of Logotherapy, Abilene, TX).

Maslow, A. H. (1971). *The Farther Reaches of Human Nature.* New York: The Viking Press.

May, Rollo. (1953). *Man's Search for Himself.* New York: New American Library, Inc.

Moore, Thomas. (1992). *Care of the Soul.* New York: HarperCollins Publishers, Inc.

Morgan, John. (2002). *Being Human: Perspectives on Meaning and Interpretation.* Bristol, IN: Quill Books

Naff, G. E. (2001). *Embracing Life: An Adaptation of the Logotherapeutic Principles of Viktor E. Frankl to Pastoral Counseling.* Unpublished.

O'Donohue, John. (1997). *Anam Cara.* New York: HarperCollins Publishers, Inc.

Prend, Ashley D. (1997). *Transcending Loss.* Berkley Books, New York.

Silverman, Ray and Star. (2000). *Spiritual Development through the Ten Commandments.* Philadelphia and Phoenix: Touchstone Seminars.

Smith, Huston. (1991). *The World's Religions.* San Francisco: Harper.

Takashima, Hiroshi (1977) *Psychosomatic Medicine and Logotherapy.* Berkeley, CA: Institute of Logotherapy Press.

Teilhard de Chardin, Pierre. (1964) *The Future of Man.* New York: Harper and Row.

Tillich, Paul. (1975). *Systematic Theology – Volume Two.* Chicago, IL: The University of Chicago Press.

Walsh, Roger, Vaughan, Frances (Eds.) (1980). *Beyond Ego: Transpersonal Dimensions in Psychology.* Los Angeles, CA: Jeremy P. Tarcher, Inc.

Wawrytko, Sandra A. (Ed.) (1980). *Analecta Frankliana: The Proceedings of the First World Congress of Logotherapy.* Berkeley, CA: Institute of Logotherapy Press.

Welter, Paul R. (1987). *Counseling and the Search for Meaning.* Word Books Publisher, Waco, TX.

Welter, Paul R. (1984). *Learning from Children.* Tyndale House Publishing, Inc., Wheaton, IL.

Welter, Paul R. (1990). *How to Help a Friend* (Revised Edition). Tyndale House Publishing, Inc., Wheaton, IL.

Weisskopf-Joelson, Edith. (1988). *Father, Have I Kept My Promise?* West Lafayette, IN: Purdue University Press.

Whitson, Robley. (1987). *The Center Scriptures.* Bristol, IN: The United Institute.

Wilson, Andew (Ed.). (1995). *World Scriptures: A Comparative Anthology of Sacred Texts.* St. Paul: Paragon House.

Yogananda, Pramahansa. (1979). *Autobiography of a Yogi.* Los Angeles, CA: Self-Realization Fellowship.

INDEX

ABOUT THE AUTHOR

Ann V. Graber grew up in Europe and was educated in Austria. As a young adult she immigrated to the US and became a naturalized citizen. After rearing her family, she continued her higher education, culminating in the Diplomate credential from the Viktor Frankl Institute of Logotherapy. She joined the Institute as a professional member and served as instructor. Her particular contribution to the Institute has been the "Distance Learning" initiative, and assisting in the development of an English language curriculum in Franklian psychology.

Searching for greater spiritual understanding, and how to implement it in service to others, led Ann to study at the Graduate Theological Foundation where she earned a D.Min. in Pastoral Counseling and, subsequently, the Ph.D. degree in Pastoral Psychology. Dr. Graber was happy to join her alma mater as professor of psychology.

A frequent presenter at conferences, Ann Graber has facilitated numerous workshops and originated seminars for diverse audiences. Her articles and writings have been published in *The International Forum for Logotherapy*, *The Chrysalis Reader*, *GTF Faculty Monograph (2004)* and have been posted on the Internet.

In her private life, Ann enjoys family, friends and colleagues. Her many interests include reading, classical music, flowers, and the finer things in life.

ᘓ